GOREN's

MODERN
BACKGAMMON
COMPLETE

GOREN'S

MODERN

BACKGAMMON

COMPLETE

Chas H Goren

A *Chancellor Hall* BOOK *published by*

DOUBLEDAY & COMPANY, NEW YORK

TECHNICAL CONSULTANT:

Charles Papazian

Library of Congress Catalogue No.: 73-14120

ISBN: 0-385-01014-1

Designed and produced by Chancellor Hall.
Printed in the United States of America

Contents

Backgammon Equipment

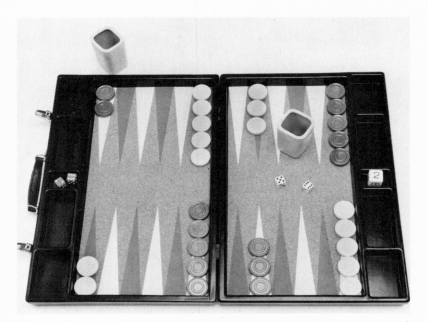

A BACKGROUND BOARD or layout.

30 round stones, tiles, or checkers, referred to throughout this book as "men." (15 each of two different colors.)

DICE: A pair of cubes with faces bearing from one to six pips. (One pair will suffice, but for speed and convenience it is customary to use two pairs, preferably of different colors.)

A DICE CUP in which to shake and from which to cast the dice. Again, for convenience, it is best to have two cups, one for each player.

A DOUBLING CUBE: A six-faced die, marked with numerals 2, 4, 8, 16, 32 and 64, to keep track of the number of points at stake in each game, as well as the player who has last doubled.

Foreword

BACKGAMMON is so ancient that none can say exactly when it was originated; traces of similar games go back as far as five thousand years. It has persisted throughout the millennia because it is fast, exciting and fun; because it is a gambler's paradise—a game that seems to be controlled by the luck of the dice, but actually involves a high degree of skill; because it can be played for family entertainment as well as for high stakes.

I intend to prove in this book that backgammon is a simple game that can be quickly learned. It is an enthralling game because a single cast of the dice can turn imminent disaster into sure victory. Yet the more skillful player is bound to win in the long run — as may be readily demonstrated if two players of unequal skill play simultaneous games, each taking his own rolls on one board and his opponent's on the other. (Remember this when your defeated opponent wails that you have had all the luck.)

After so many centuries, what has caused the sudden, dramatic surge in the popularity of modern backgammon? There are many theories. I do not share the view that gambling games reflect the spirit of our times. I believe that families have discovered backgammon's fascination; discovered that it can be played with children or as a husband-and-wife game; that, while essentially a game for two, any number can actively participate; that it can be played for a few minutes or for hours at a time.

Whatever the reasons, backgammon has burst forth from its enduring popularity as a side game played at posh clubs to its rightful place as a sport; a sport with just the right mixture of luck and skill to fascinate those who love to play for high stakes and, equally, those who play for pennies, peanuts or just plain pleasure.

For new players

The easiest, quickest and most enjoyable way to learn any game is by playing it. The best way to improve is to decide how you would play; then have an expert tell you exactly what you should have done and why.

That is the plan of this book.

We will take the mystery out of the unfamiliar-looking board; tell you how the game is played and won; what the simple basic strategies are and what are the best moves for every possible opening throw. Immediately after that, you begin playing actual games. You can do so right in this book, without reference to a board. (However, I strongly recommend that you have a board handy, set up the men and make each play as you go along. You might even chalk the point numbers onto your board until you become familiar with them.)

You will be given a chance to decide how you'd play each throw. Then you'll be allowed to make the best move. You can even do the same thing with your opponent's moves (White's), although in the beginning it may be less confusing to play your side of the board only. The basic strategies will be explained as you play them out. You'll be playing with an expert sitting beside you to confirm your play or suggest another.

That's why this book has 213 diagrams — more than any other book on backgammon; why it starts simply and goes winging along in a way that teaches you all the right moves while you are playing.

For those who have played before

Pretty soon, even if you start as a beginner, you'll feel at home in this more advanced category. And if you have already played more or less often, you'll find yourself increasing your skill at a rapid pace; soon you'll be ready to take on anyone who isn't already an expert.

For the expert

Backgammon strategy has changed more in the past few years than in all the centuries it was played before the evolution of the modern game. Moves that every expert would have considered as "automatic" as recently as a year or so ago have been exposed as less effective than the new and more daring gambits introduced by the modern, younger experts. Many of the old-time champions have now accepted these ideas, discarding the older, more conservative moves.

This book brings you the most modern advice; advice with which you can defeat your fellow experts unless they, too, have learned the superior stratagems of modern backgammon.

Acknowledgements

Many experts, both at backgammon itself and at explaining a game so that learning becomes simple, have contributed materially to the preparation of this book. I particularly wish to acknowledge the invaluable assistance of my technical consultant, Charles Papazian, who is today considered one of the finest of the modern backgammon experts.

I would also like to thank Harold Feldheim, Harold Ogust and Richard L. Frey for helping me to make this book meet the goal I set: to be the best and at the same time the easiest-to-follow book ever written about this fascinating and challenging game, which has always been one of my special favorites.

Charles H. Goren

Miami Beach, Nov. 1973

I Introduction to Backgammon and its strategy

THOUGH you may never have played backgammon, you have probably seen (perhaps on the back of a checkerboard) the odd-looking layout of 24 "daggers," twelve on one side pointing directly across to twelve on the other. Don't let these daggers mystify you. In fact, each is merely a division of the track for an obstacle race between two 15-man teams.

Instead of these triangular points, if the track were made up of rectangular spaces familiar to you in playing such games as parchesi, snakes and ladders, or Monopoly, it might be easier for you to recognize the course over which the race is run.

So, as our first illustration, we have drawn the layout in this way, with arrows to indicate the direction in which each player's men will race along the track.

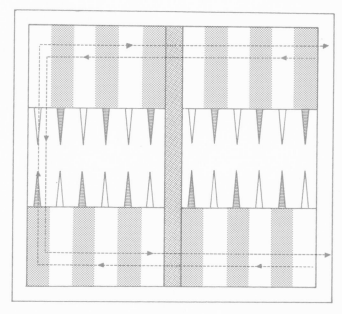

Throughout this book, you will always be seated at the bottom side of the board, playing the Red men. Your opponent, seated across the table, will be moving his men, the Whites, in the opposite direction.

As shown by the diagram, the backgammon layout is divided in half by the "bar" — a central partition running down the middle — into an *outer* and *inner* (or *home*) *board* or *table*. Each half of the layout is further divided: the side away from you is *his* inner or outer table; the side nearer you is *your* inner or outer table. (It is equally correct to call this the inner or outer *board*.) These divisions are largely for the purpose of convenient reference, although the term "home" board relates to the fact that you must bring *all* your men home as the penultimate step toward winning the game.

Of course in an actual game you may be playing from the other side, so I suggest you turn the diagram upside down (look at the next diagram this way, too) viewing the board as your opponent sees it. Note that it will always be true of each player that his men travel from 1 to 12 across the opposite side — the top — of the board; then they move back from 12 toward 1 on the side of the board nearest him.

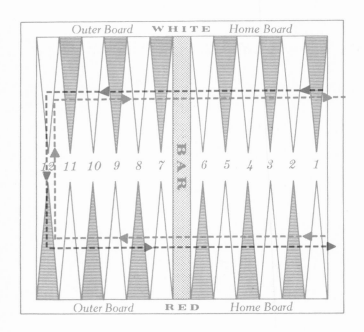

The move from the 12-point on one side of the board to the 12-point on the other is only a single step, the same as the move from spaces — in backgammon, they are called "points" — that are next to one another.

The numbers on the diagrams do not appear on an actual board. However, they are used throughout the book — and very often during the play of a game — to describe a particular move or position. Your (Red's) 3-point or 5-point will always be on your side of the board; "his" (White's) points will always be the corresponding number on his side of the board.

Don't worry if you do not immediately learn to recognize the number for each point. They will soon become familiar. Meanwhile, if you are setting up a board and playing each move as you read (a very good idea if the board is convenient), you may find it helpful to lightly chalk in the numbers as suggested earlier.

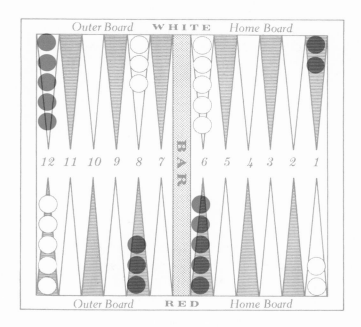

Here is the backgammon board, set up with both sides' men in place, ready to start play. Note that only the two men stationed on the 1-point — called "runners" — will have to traverse the entire length of the track. The others are posted on four "relay" stations along the way. These stations or "points" are "owned" by the player whose men occupy them and will continue to be controlled by that player as long as at least two of his men remain posted there. They provide safe landing places for his men as well as blockade points against his opponent's moves. The more such points you can control by occupying them with at least two men, the more difficult it becomes for your opponent to bring his men around the board and the safer it is for you to do so.

OBJECT OF THE GAME

To bring all of your men around the track and into your inner (home) board. (See diagram.) Then to remove them from the board. (See "Bearing off.") The first to get all of his men off the board is the winner.

COMMENCING THE GAME

Each player casts one die. High plays first, using the combined result of the two dice as his throw for his opening move.* If each throws the same number, both roll again until different numbers appear. (In some games, it is customary to consider each tie throw as an "automatic double," so that the doubling cube is advanced to 2, then 4, then 8 should tie throws continue. However, most games limit such automatic doubles to one or two, and many games — including those played in tournaments — simply ignore the tie and roll again.)

MOVES

Each player's turn consists of moving one or more of his men in accordance with the numbers resulting from a cast of two dice. The move may be taken by one or more men. However, even when taken with a single man, the move is not the sum total of the pips on both dice but the separate moving of a man the exact number of spaces dictated by each individual die. Thus, if your throw is 5–4 you do not count it as a 9, as you would in other games; you may move one man four points and another five, or you may move five and four with a single man.

You cannot move a man whose progress — as dictated by the number of pips on each die — would require it to touch down, either in passing or at the end of the move, on a point where your opponent already has two or more men. To avoid this, you may count your man's progression using either number first, and you may pass over as many such enemy-controlled points as the

* VARIANT: Some play that this cast merely determines the player who has the first turn. That player then throws his two dice to decide his opening move.

4

number on a single die allows without touching down on one of them. You may land, or touch down in passing, on any point that you control, or that is open, or that is occupied by only one of your opponent's men. In fact, in this last case, it will usually be to your advantage to do so. (See "Blots".)

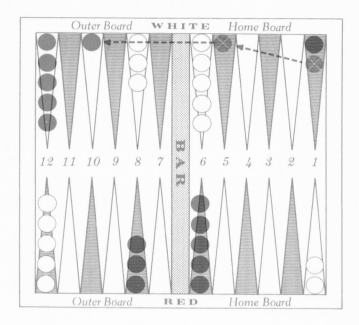

Returning to consideration of your hypothetical opening throw of 5–4, if you were compelled to take the higher number first you could not move a runner from White's 1-point because White owns the 6-point. However, you are *not* required to move in a particular order, so you can take a man first to White's 5-point, then out to his 10-point.

But if White had played first and made his 5-point, as for example by using a 3–1 to bring men from his 8-point ·and his 6-point, you would be unable to move your runners and would have to choose some other man or men with which to take your 5–4.

DOUBLETS

When you throw the same number on both dice, as 1–1, 4–4, etc., instead of taking that number twice you take it four times. Thus, 4–4, for example, is taken in four progressions of four points each and may be taken with one, two, three or four men.

5

Throwing a doublet provides several possible advantages. By increasing the number of spaces you are to travel, it helps in the race to bring your men around the board as rapidly as possible, called a *running game*. More important, it enables you to move men in pairs, allowing you to make new points as blockades against your opponent and also to provide safe landing places for your own men.

COUNTING YOUR MOVE

As a hint to help you count out your moves: You will have noticed that the points are of alternating tones. An even number will always move a man to a point of the same hue as the one he leaves; an odd number will move to a different color. A throw of six will always carry your man to the corresponding position in the next *quadrant* of the board. As previously noted, these quadrants are created by the *bar* — a panel running across the board between the 6-point and the 7-point, or "*bar-point.*" When moving your men, the bar itself does not count as a space. It simply separates the board into inner and outer tables, most often referred to as your or your opponent's "inner board" or "outer board."

It is customary for each player to roll his dice in his own right-hand board. (See "Cocked Dice.")

MAKING POINTS

A player *makes* a point whenever he places two or more of his men upon it. The advantage of making points is that each such point provides a safe resting place for your own men and at the same time acts as a blockade against the opposing men. A player may not touch down on a point controlled by his opponent, nor may two players of the same side occupy the same point.

BLOTS

A single man left on a point is called a blot. If you are able to move a man onto an opponent's blot, or to touch down on it in the course of moving one man for the distance dictated by the two dice of your throw, the blot is *hit* and is removed from the table.

A blot that has been hit is placed "on the bar." This is the equivalent of "sending him home" to start all over again, so it is usually to your advantage to hit an opponent's blot.

6

RE-ENTERING FROM THE BAR

A player who has one or more men *on the bar* must re-enter them before he can make any other move. Re-entry must be made on the opponent's home table, using the number shown on one die in that throw. Of course you may not re-enter on a point that has been made by your opponent; you may come in on an open point, or on a point occupied by your own man or men, or on one occupied by an opponent's single man, in which last case you will have hit his blot and put *his* man on the bar.

If you can re-enter with either of the numbers on your dice, you may choose which one to use. If only one number will bring you in, you *must* use it and then take the other number in any legal way, provided you no longer have a man on the bar. Until you have brought all your men off the bar, you may not make any other play. For example, if you are so unfortunate as to throw 6–6 while on the bar, your man will remain there because your opponent controls the 6-point (see previous diagram). Thus you will have lost your turn.

CLOSED BOARD

When you have made all six points on your inner table you have closed your board. If your opponent has a man on the bar, it will be impossible for him to re-enter. In this situation, you alone continue to cast your dice and play until such time as you are forced to open up a point on which he may re-enter.

PRIME

A player who has made six consecutive points anywhere on the board has completed a *prime*. An opposing man caught behind a prime cannot move beyond it, because the largest single number he can throw is a 6. Nevertheless, the owner of the trapped man continues to throw in his turn and to make all moves as are possible.

COMPULSORY MOVE

A player must take all of his move if there is any possible way for him to do so. If he is unable to take all of it, he must take as much of it as possible. If he can move only half of his throw, he must take the larger number if it is legal to do so. A player cannot pass his turn, except when he is on the bar against a closed board.

7

BEARING OFF

As soon as you have moved all fifteen of your men into your home board, you may commence *bearing off*. This is the final stage of the race. Once borne off the table, that man never returns to play. The first player to remove all fifteen men is the winner. Note, however, that you may not bear off while any of your men remain outside your home board or on the bar. Thus, if a blot should be hit while you are bearing off, you must re-enter your man and bring him back to your home board before you resume the process of bearing off. Once your man has re-entered, you may, however, use the rest of your throw to move men *within* your home board in preference to bringing him around toward home.

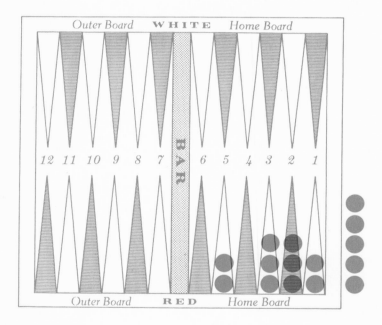

In bearing off, just as in earlier play, you must move your men in accordance with the numbers of each throw whenever you are legally able to do so. Thus, in the diagram above after you have borne off five men your position is as shown.

If your throw is 5–3: You may take off the board one man from your 5-point and one from your 3-point.

> RULE: *You may bear off a man whenever his position on the board corresponds to the number that appears on a die.*

However, if your opponent still has a man on the bar, you will not want to take the move as suggested, leaving two blots, so you will bear one man off the 5-point and use the 3 to move the second man from the 5-point to your 2-point.

> RULE: *You may use any or all of your roll to move men within your home board instead of bearing them off.*

If your *throw* is *6–1*: You do not have a man on your 6-point, so you must use the 6 to take a man off the highest numbered point you occupy. If your opponent does not have a man on the bar, or in a position deep in your inner board, you will use the 1 to remove a man from your 1-point. But if he has a man on the bar or on your 4-point you will have to leave a blot. If his man is on the 4-point, you will use the 1 to bear off a man from your 1-point. If he is on the bar, you will move the second man from your 5-point to your 4-point, leaving only one blot for him to hit.

> RULE: *The roll of a number higher than your highest occupied point must be applied to the man on the latter point. However, you always have the privilege of moving a lower number first.*

For further pointers in bearing off, see Chapter v.

GAMMON AND BACKGAMMON

If you are able to remove all 15 of your men from the board before your opponent has removed a single man, you have scored a *gammon*, worth twice the value of that game. If you bear off all your men while your opponent has a man in your home board (or on the bar) and before he has borne off a single man, you score a *back-gammon*, worth three times the value of that game.

COCKED DICE

The two dice must be thrown together and must come to rest flat on the surface of the table at your right. If one die moves into the other table, or off the board, or is not completely flat on the board, this constitutes cocked dice and the player must roll again.

If you are impatient to start playing at once, you may skip the rest of this chapter for the time being and move right along to playing the opening moves, as explained in Chapter ii. However, you will better understand the reasons for these moves and the basic idea of the game if you follow through first with the underlying principles.

GENERAL STRATEGY

From what you have read thus far, you may have gained the impression that the winning plan is to move your men around the track as rapidly and as safely as possible at all times, advancing your men so as to leave as few blots as possible. Wrong!

That is the usual plan adopted by the inexperienced player and, barring a series of miraculous throws, it is almost a sure way to lose!

Remember in the first paragraph of this chapter we defined backgammon as an *obstacle race*. Therefore, the surest way to win is to construct the strongest possible obstacles against the progress of your opponent. As a first illustration, let's return to playing a throw of 5–4, discussed earlier under the heading of *Moves*. Here is a later development of the situation in which you cannot move one of your runners with a 5–4 because White has made his 5-point.

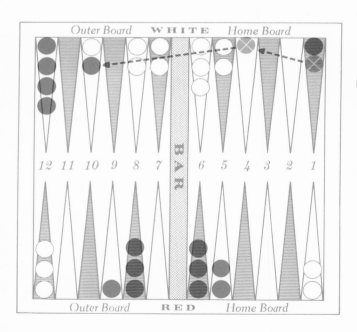

The man on White's 10-point is exactly nine points away from the Red runners, yet you cannot hit this blot because both the 4 and the 5 land on points that are owned by White. (Remember, whenever you have two or more men on a point, your opponent may not land there.)

Let's assume, however, that instead of 5–4 you have rolled 6–3. The total of nine is just the same, but now you can hit the blot. You can move a runner from your 1-point three points to the unoccupied White 4-point; then you can easily leap over White's blockade with the 6, hitting the blot. You always have the option of determining which of the two numbers of your throw you wish to play first.

The next diagram illustrates the position after you hit White's blot with 6–3.

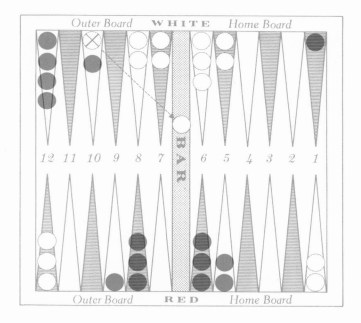

By hitting the blot, you have placed your man on the 10-point and put White's man on the bar. At his next turn, before he can make any other play, White must re-enter his man from the bar to a point designated by one of the numbers of his throw.

Assume his next throw is 6–4. He may not come in on the 6-point because you own it. Therefore, he *must* re-enter his man on your 4-point. Now he may move any legal 6 with any man he wishes.

But suppose White had rolled 6–5 instead of 6–4. You control both the 6-point and the 5-point so White's man would remain on the bar and he would lose his turn. Remember, a player must re-enter all men on the bar before he can make any other play.

Control of points serves two valuable purposes. First, they provide your men with safe landing places for their trip around the board. But even more important, as you saw in the previous discussion, the points you own inhibit or block an opponent's movements — sometimes, as when he is on the bar, so that he cannot move at all.

To establish the most effective blockade, you should try to make your points in sequence. The most effective sequence is a *prime* (six points in a row), which traps any man behind it. To emphasize the importance of building a blockade, let's skip for the moment to a late stage of the game. Consider White's plight in the following diagram.

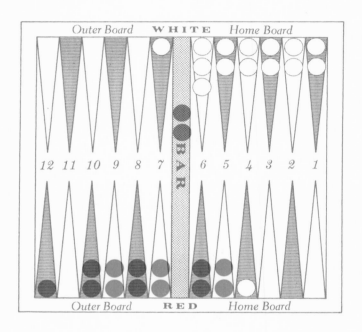

It appears that White has an overwhelming advantage. The two Red men on the bar cannot re-enter, because all of White's home board is closed. Yet White, not Red, has the losing position. White's man in your home board is trapped behind a prime. No number he can roll will allow him to move this man, and you can't even throw, so your prime is sure to endure until White is forced to open points on his home board and you have brought both your men in. Eventually, you will re-enter your two men, bring them around the board and by advancing your prime you will win the game. Here's the same game, eight rolls later:

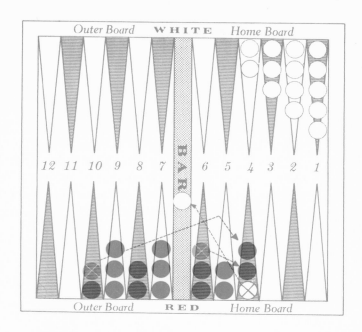

CLOSING YOUR BOARD

You have re-entered your men after White was forced to break up his home board. White's blot on your 4-point is helpless. Your object is to make the 4-point, hitting his blot and simultaneously advancing your prime. You might do this if your next roll were 6–2, moving a man from your 10-point and another from your 6-point as shown by the arrows. Your next objectives are to make the 3-point, then the 2-point, then the 1-point, doing so in that order so as to maintain your prime. Then you can begin to bear men off the board while White looks on helplessly until you break up your home board. By this time, however, you should have removed one or more men and White will be far behind.

The process of making the points in your board successively while closing your board is called a moving prime or, sometimes, a "caterpillar." Re-examine the previous diagram and notice that even if you had failed to throw a number to make your 4-point, you should hit White's man on that point, leaving a blot. As long as you maintain your prime, it will do no harm if your blot is hit. You may re-enter White's home board at your leisure — perhaps even hit another blot — and try again, always posting a man on the point directly ahead of your prime as soon as you possibly can. White's man continues to be trapped and must meekly await his fate.

13

Let us assume that you have been successful in closing your board as in the following diagram.

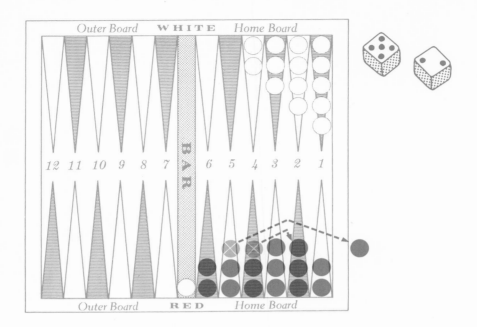

White has been closed out. His man cannot re-enter from the bar until you open a point for him. Having brought all fifteen men into your home board, you are now ready to begin *bearing off*. If you were in a straight race and White had no man threatening to hit any blot you might leave, you would utilize each throw to bear off as many men as possible. But in this case, you must be careful not to leave a blot that might be hit by White's man on the bar.

You roll 5–2. Do not remove a man from the 5- and another from the 2-point. To avoid leaving a blot, you bear off a man from the 5-point and move a man from the 4-point to the 2-point, as shown. Since your board remains closed and no throw would let White's man enter, you throw again, rolling 6–4. Still being careful to avoid leaving a blot, you bear off a man from the 6-point and move the other man from that point to your 2-point.

With a point now available for re-entry, White gets a throw and rolls 6–5, allowing him to re-enter immediately and run out to the 11-point, reaching this position:

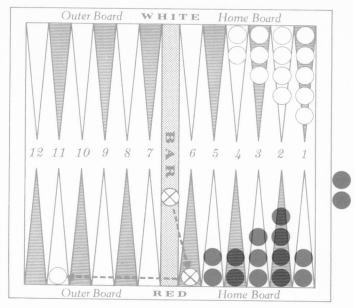

Though White was lucky to be able to re-enter quickly, his race is virtually hopeless. It is your roll. You will certainly bear off two more men. White has yet to bring his man into his home board before he can even begin to bear off. Leaving aside consideration of doublets, you should be able to bear off all your men in seven rolls, while it will take White at least nine. Two long strides is a pretty impressive lead toward the end of a track race.

Let's take this opportunity to summarize the basic principles to be followed in bearing off:

1] If no enemy man is either in your home board or on the bar, bear off your men as *quickly* as possible.

2] If an enemy man is in your home board or on the bar, bear off as *safely* as possible, to avoid leaving a blot.

THE KEY POINTS

Unfortunately, Lady Luck does not always provide the precise throws needed to construct a prime, so in the early game we must concentrate on trying to gain control of key blocking points that may eventually lead to a prime or to winning without establishing one.

15

Two points are of great strategical value — your 7-point, called the bar-point, and your 5-point.

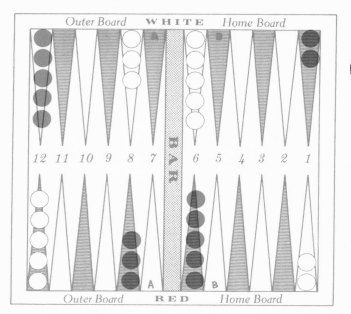

The runners, the men who start on each side's opponent's 1-point, have to make the longest and most hazardous trip around the board. Therefore, your earliest attempts *at blocking action* should be directed against the opposing runners. By constructing either your 5-point or your bar-point, you begin this blockade. The bar-point (A) gives you three contiguous points, the rudiments of a prime. It also blocks good running numbers, such as 6–6, or the 6–5 throw that would otherwise allow your opponent to bring one of his runners to immediate safety on the 12-point. As an example, notice how a run to safety with 6-5 would be blocked because both the 6- and 5-points are controlled by your opponent.

The 5-point (B) also serves to block running numbers for your opponent — 4–4 or 5–4 — and gives you two consecutive points in your home board. This is important for the additional reason that each point you establish in your home board makes it more and more hazardous for your opponent to leave a blot. The more points you close, the greater the likelihood that, if hit, he will not be able to re-enter; the nearer these points are to the bar, the more difficult it will be for his runners to escape.

16

Both the bar-point and the 5-point are also excellent landing places for your men. If you are able to capture these points early, you will have gained a tremendous advantage.

If you cannot build either of these points, the next best thing is to threaten to occupy your opponent's bar-point or 5-point. Obviously, if it is good for him to make a key point, it must be good for you to prevent his making it, and the best way to accomplish that is to make the point yourself.

BLOTS: DANGERS vs ADVANTAGES

No doubt you have come to the conclusion that hitting an opponent's blot is good strategy. You are right, although it does not necessarily follow that it is always your best move.

However, since backgammon is a race, when you hit a blot the opponent loses whatever ground that piece has gained because it must return to the start of the track and begin all over again. Add to this advantage the fact that your opponent may be unable to throw a number that will enable him to re-enter on the next roll, or that in order to do so he will lose the advantage of what otherwise might have been a very helpful combination.

Despite these dangers, it is often correct strategy to leave blots; in fact, much of the skill in backgammon is concerned with the placement of blots as threats to the opposition and as potential *builders*. The time to take risks is early in the game when both sides are still attempting to establish a position.

We have already discussed the value of making points, and especially the key points. However, aside from doublets, there are only four* throws that can be used to make these key points from the original set-up of your men: 6–1 and 3–1. Sooner or later, barring miracles, you will have to leave blots. The earlier you do this, the safer it is — because your opponent will not yet have established many points in his board — and the more valuable your blot will be as a potential builder of one of the key points. Consider the point-making possibilities of the next diagram.

---

* For purposes of this book, a non-doublet throw is always represented "higher number first," but the reader should bear in mind that each non-doublet really represents two combinations: 6–1 and 1–6, for example. Of the possible rolls, the six doublets represent single chances; the fifteen non-doublets represent double chances. In comparing total chances, the non-doublet is therefore counted twice, and the total possibility is 30 plus 6 or 36.

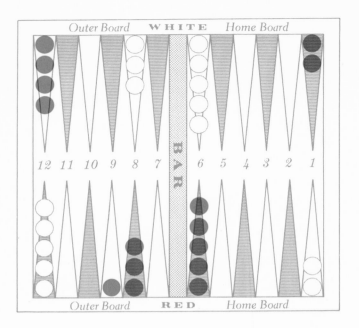

This diagram is almost the position of the men at the beginning of the game; the difference is that we've moved one of your men from White's 12-point to your 9-point. (Disregard the fact that this would not have been the correct move for a throw that would lead to such a position. For the moment, we are concerned only with comparing the dangers and the advantages of this blot.)

White can hit it with any of six numbers (4–4, 2–2 — single chances — and 5–3, 6–2 — double chances). Against this risk, you have increased by eight your possibilities for making one of the key points. Using the blot on the 9-point if it survives to your next throw, you can build either the bar-point or the 5-point with twelve numbers instead of the original four. Instead of being makable only with 6–1, the bar point may now be made with 2–1 or 6–2. The 5-point can be made not only with 3–1, but with 4–3 or 4–1. (For your own practice, move the men to see how each of these points is made.) To repeat: six numbers endanger your blot, while eight increase its usefulness.

RULE: *Whenever a blot can produce more useful numbers than the numbers by which it can be hit, it is a well-placed blot.*

This plan of placing well-calculated blots is called *diversification* or *flexibility*, and will be more fully discussed later.

18

Choice of game plans

THE RUNNING GAME

The *straight race* or the *non-contact race*, usually called the running game, is the simplest plan, although not by any means the most often chosen. Typically, a running game occurs when both sides are able to bring their runners to safety during the early stages of the play. Consider this position:

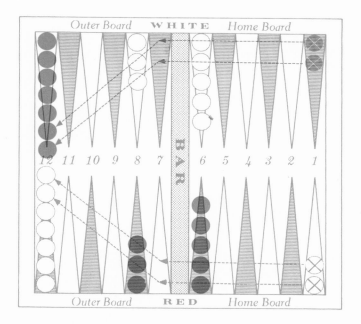

Each player has made two moves, and by an unlikely coincidence both rolled 6–5 twice, bringing their runners to safety. A similar position might have been reached if both had thrown 6–4 twice, or if one had thrown 6–5 twice and the other 6–4 twice, using that throw to bring his two runners to the opposing 11-point. Neither side will leave the other a blot to hit and the game will be won by the player who thereafter throws the larger numbers or, occasionally when the numbers are roughly equal, by the player whose throws result in the best deployment of men in his home board.

From a strategical point of view, there is little interest left in such a game. Each side will try to bring his men home as quickly and as economically as possible so as to exercise the greatest speed and economy in bearing off. It is fortunate for backgammon's popularity that such games occur infrequently. (For a full Straight Race Game, see page 131.)

THE POSITIONAL OR BLOCKING GAME

This is the most frequent and the most challenging game type. Each side is trying to restrict or contain the other's men while trying to retain mobility for his own. Both sides have made points, deployed their forces to take utmost advantage of their throws, and are battling for position. The following diagram illustrates a late position in a positional or blocking game.

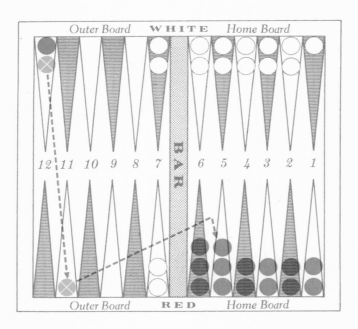

The position illustrated is called "juxtaposed bars." Both sides have imposing positions in their home boards. White is behind in the race and needs a large double to run safely off your bar-point. He would much prefer to force Red to leave a shot, as is highly likely unless you roll a double that will enable you to move your men off his 12-point and bring them both home safely.

20

Notice that if you throw a 6 with any number other than another 6 — in which case your position would be held because you cannot legally move a man 6 points — you will be forced to move a man from the 12-point as there are no other 6-moves available. Your actual throw, 6–2, leaves you no choice. In order to take this number you must first move a 2 to the 11 point and then a 6 with the same man, as shown by the dotted line in the diagram. White will have just about an even chance to hit your blot (17 numbers hit; 19 numbers miss), and if he succeeds he will almost certainly win the game. (For examples of exciting positional games see pages 144 and 154.)

A distinguishing characteristic of the positional or blocking game is that either side may win and both players must maneuver with considerable skill to maximize their chances. At an earlier stage, this skill would include trying to maintain flexibility, if necessary making some daring moves in an attempt to equalize the position, with the thought in mind that if you are unsuccessful you can shift your plan to the third game type:

THE BACK GAME

This is the most delicate strategy to plan and execute, although when it is properly timed it can put the player who is seemingly far behind in the race in a position so advantageous that he is more likely to win than his opponent.

Usually you will be forced to plan a back game when two or more of your blots have been hit during the opening stages, giving your opponent a formidable lead in a straight race. To overcome this, your hope is to hold two or more points deep in your opponent's home board, waiting for him to leave an opportune blot, which is extremely likely unless he is very lucky in his throws. Meanwhile, however, you must not allow your other men to become so far advanced that before you get the shot you will have had to break up your home board. The following diagram illustrates a late middle-game position in which you have set up an effective backgame structure.

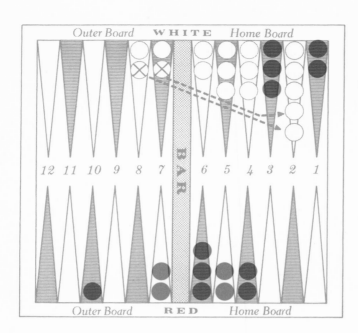

White is substantially ahead in the race, but he was bound to have an awkward time bringing his men home safely. His actual throw of 6–5 was a major disaster because his only legal plays, as illustrated by the diagram, leave two blots exposed to attack from two different Red points. You are a heavy favorite to hit one of the blots on your next throw; only if you fail to throw a 6, 5 or 4 on either die would you miss — 27 chances in your favor to 9 against. This, plus your well-deployed home board — not to mention the possibility that you might hit both blots — means that you now have by far the best chance to win the game.

Even if White had not left a shot on this roll, it is very likely that he would soon be forced to leave a *double shot* (that is, a blot subject to a direct hit by either of two men). The cornerstone of your success in this game was timing. You had to be careful — and to a certain extent lucky to avoid doublets — not to bring your men around the board too quickly. Otherwise, you would have had to break up your home board before you got a chance to hit White. Had this happened, a potential shot would no longer be a serious threat. To illustrate, if you were White would you be afraid to leave a shot in this back game which Red has timed quite badly in the following diagram?

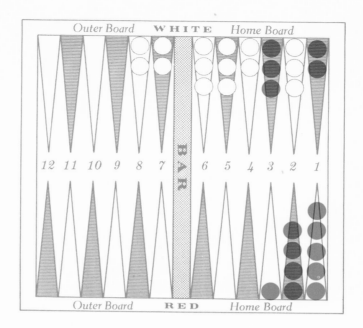

12 11 10 9 8 7 **BAR** 6 5 4 3 2 1

Red's home board is no longer a blockading threat and White need have no great fear of leaving a blot.

The general strategy of a back game is to move around the track as slowly as possible. To do this, it may be often necessary for you to entice or compel White to slow you up by hitting one or more blots. White, being aware of your aims, will avoid hitting blots unnecessarily, hoping that you will be forced to break up your home board prematurely.

A successful back game position, such as in the properly timed diagram shown earlier, is a slight favorite to win the game, even before the disaster met by White with his throw of 6–5. BUT, and it is a big *but*, when a back game player loses he is in grave danger of being *gammoned* (paying double stakes) and may even be *backgammoned*, losing a triple game. For this reason, one does not deliberately strive for a back game, but keeps it in reserve as a winning possibility to fall back on after many of your blots· have been hit in the opening stages. (To follow a well-played back game, see page 166.)

ii The opening moves

AS YOU KNOW, to start the game, the player who throws the higher number on a single die gains the privilege of making the first move. At the beginning, the board is a battlefield with equal armies opposing each other from identical positions. From the first roll onwards the men begin to move guided by your decisions. Your method of deployment, even more than the luck of the dice, will be the main determinant of your success or failure. If any phase of the game is of primary importance, the opening is that phase. Entire games can be won or lost based on decisions made in the early stages of play. In this section we are going to determine the best opening move for each throw. It is not our purpose to test your ability to memorize moves, although you would do well to familiarize yourself with these openings. The major reason for this analysis is to acquaint you with some basic strategical considerations, particularly the use of well-placed blots as builders toward making key points, as touched upon in Chapter i.

An important fact to remember is that *it is always an advantage to make the first move*, and since certain opening rolls are better than others, we will evaluate the quality of a particular throw as being excellent, over average, under average or poor. Even a poor throw confers some advantage although that advantage may be minimal. For our purposes, the opening rolls will be divided into three sections.

1] THE AUTOMATIC ROLL — *Moves which produce an immediate and tangible positional gain. There are four automatic rolls.*

2] THE STRATEGIC ROLL — *Moves which require the placement of blots as builders in the hopes of future positional gains. There are eleven strategic rolls.*

3] THE DOUBLET ROLL* — *Moves which almost always produce*

* *A doublet roll, of course, can be played only as the opening roll of the second player, since duplicated numbers on the first throw of a single die necessitate rolling again to determine who plays first.*

24

a tangible gain in the race, in point making, or both. There
are six doublet rolls.

Although the diagrams should be easy to follow, it would be to your advantage to set up your own backgammon board and play the moves whenever a board is handy.

Again let me remind you that, for the sake of uniformity, it is assumed that you are playing the Red men.

THE AUTOMATIC ROLL confers an immediate advantage. In each case, it will be readily apparent how your deployment has been improved. These rolls are referred to as "automatic" simply because the recommended move is obviously of such advantage that it is the only acceptable move. Note, in each case, how these moves tend to point up your next objectives.

The automatic rolls

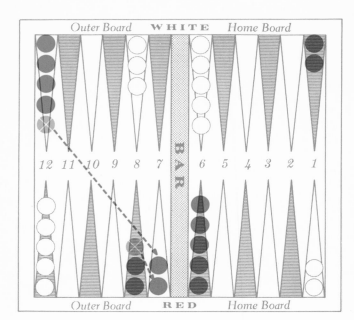

6 – 1

Move a man from the White 12-point to your bar-point.

Move a man from your 8-point to your bar-point.

The 6–1 is one of the two best opening throws. You have made one of the two key strategic blocking points — the bar-point, as illustrated. By controlling three points in a row, you have constructed the beginnings of an effective blockade against the White runners.

Future plans should be aimed at further restricting the mobility of the opposing runners by making your 5-point or 4-point. To carry out this plan, builders should be brought into your outer board either as blots or to the safety of the bar-point or the 8-point. In later moves you will see that while blots are often builders, builders do not necessarily have to be blots.

3 – 1

Move a man from the 8-point to the 5-point.

Move a man from the 6-point to the 5-point.

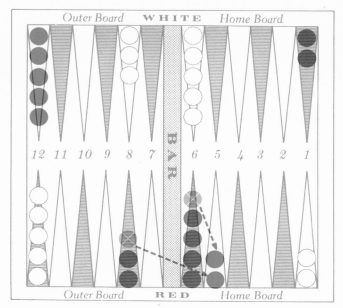

The 3–1 is the second of the two best opening numbers. As with the 6–1, you have made one of the two key strategic blocking points — in this case, the 5-point. The 5-point serves the triple function of inhibiting the movement of the White runners, making the most valuable point in your home board and providing a safe landing spot for builders of future home board points.

Future deployment should be aimed at making the bar-point to further restrict the White runners. As soon as possible, at least one builder should be moved to your outer board; if you are able to make the bar-point quickly, your positional advantage will be close to decisive. On this basis, it is worth some risk to increase your potential to construct this important point. If convenient, a builder should also be brought to your 5-point, aiming toward later making the 4-point.

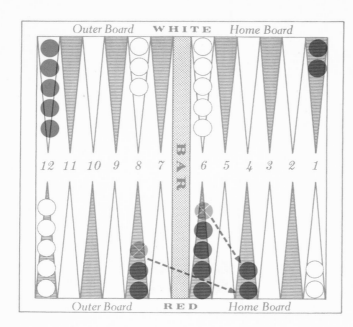

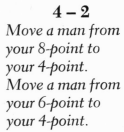

4 – 2
Move a man from your 8-point to your 4-point. Move a man from your 6-point to your 4-point.

The 4–2 makes your 4-point, as illustrated. While not as good as either 6–1 or 3–1, this number may be counted among the excellent first rolls.

The 4-point is a good strategic point to own because of its proximity to the 5-point and the bar-point. In our analysis of both the 6–1 and the 3–1, the 4-point was recommended as an objective when considering future strategy. By itself, the 4-point does not really do very much. It is in conjunction with either the 5-point or the bar-point that its restrictive qualities begin to loom large. Logically, therefore, our future strategy should be based on constructing either of the two key points. If your next throw is 3–1, you will of course make the 5-point. If it is 6–1, you will make the bar-point. Do not be concerned that both of these moves leave a blot on the 8-point. Except when obviously more advantageous moves may be made, single pieces should be moved to your outer board as soon as possible to serve as builders.

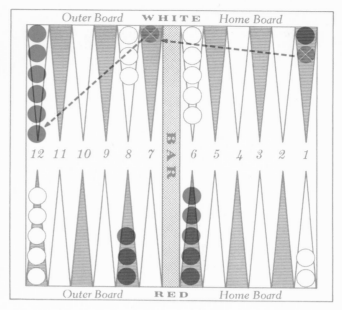

6 – 5

Move a runner to the White bar-point.
Continue with the same runner to the White 12-point.

This move to safety is known as "lover's leap." While seemingly unrelated, this move follows the theme of the other automatic moves.

The golden rule of backgammon may be stated, "Do unto others before they have a chance to do it unto you." Just as you have been attempting to restrict your opponents runners, your opponent (who may also be reading this book) will be trying to restrain your runners. By moving one of them to safety, you've blunted his purpose since there is only one of your men left in your opponent's home board.

This is an automatic opening roll. We do not consider it an excellent roll because, despite its good racing qualities and its safety, it does nothing to help construct points or threaten to construct points. Your future plans should involve bringing the other runner to safety and making useful points. You should not be afraid to move men to your outer board in an effort to fulfill this latter objective, since even if you do "safety" the other runner, you will soon need additional safe landing spots for your men, as well as blockade points against the opponent's runners.

It is not especially dangerous to leave a single unguarded man on your opponent's 1-point. It will inhibit his easy formation of points in his home board, and if he should hit you it will put one of his men out of position, without costing you much in the race.

The strategic rolls

UNLIKE THE AUTOMATIC ROLLS, the strategic rolls do not create such immediate tangible advantages as making points or safetying a runner. The watchword for these rolls is 'potential.' You will be advised to leave blots, even in situations where a blot can be avoided. By now, however, you realize that at this early stage blots are potential builders for future points. The effectiveness of a builder is directly related to the number of additional future rolls that let you make useful points. The dangers are directly related to the number of throws with which the builders can be hit. On each of the strategic rolls, the indicated blot is potentially more useful as a builder than it is endangered by being hit.

There are five basic strategic moves. These are:

1] THE RUNNING MOVE — *an attempt to escape with a runner.*

2] THE BUILD-UP THREAT — *bringing a builder to your outer board to increase the number of throws that will make key points.*

3] THE RUNNER SPREAD — *a move in your opponent's home board to increase the flexibility of your runners.*

4] THE GAMBLING MOVE — *leaving a direct shot (hittable with one die) on your 5-point in hopes of making that point quickly; or of bringing one of your runners to the opponent's bar-point in an attempt either to make that point or to force him to place a blot on the bar-point in order to hit you.*

5] THE COMBINATION STRATEGIES — *representing any combination of these classifications.*

If any of these categories seem vague, don't worry. They will become simple after a very few pages.

6 – 4

Move a runner to the White bar-point.

Continue with the same man to the White 11-point.

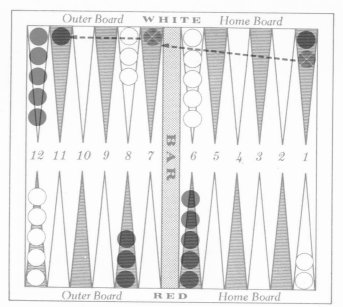

This running number, as illustrated, is an attempt to bring a runner toward safety. Unlike the 6–5, however, the runner is vulnerable to a shot. If White rolls a 2 as part of his next throw, he can hit the blot, forcing you to lose the advantage of your first turn and waste a part of your next turn by having to reenter your man in White's home board.

Does this mean that 6–4 is a worse throw than 6–5? Not necessarily. White hits the blot with eleven numbers but will miss with 25 numbers. Two of the "hit" numbers — 4–2, 2–4 — will cost him the advantage of making his 4-point. What you've lost in safety, you've gained in flexibility. Assuming that White misses, follow-up rolls such as 5–4, 4–3, or 3–2 can be used to make blocking points in your outer board; for example: 5–4 will allow you to make your 9-point with your advanced runner and a man from White's 12-point. A second 6–4 will let you cover the blot on the 11-point. As an exercise, determine how you can utilize the 4–3 to make your 10-point and the 3–2 to make your 11-point.

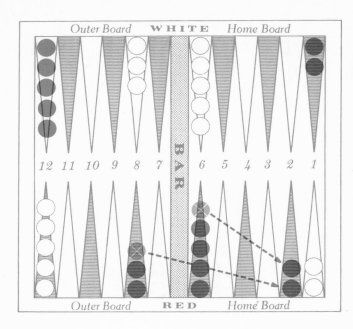

6 – 4

A poor way to play 6–4 would be to make your 2-point as illustrated.

To understand why this is a bad play despite its temporary safety, consider what you have learned about which points are valuable and why. We mentioned earlier the tremendous blockading potential of the bar-point and the 5-point against the opponent's runners. The 2-point has little blocking value because it is so far forward in your inner board; White should have little problem leaping over it.

Aside from the key points (bar-point and 5-point), the best points to make in the opening are those which are closest to the key points. Thus, as we learned earlier, the 4-point is quite good because of its proximity to the 5-point. Later in the game, the 2-point might be useful, but to the extent that it moves two men out of action in the early struggle, the 2-point is a cowardly maneuver in the opening, and likely to become a costly one.

5 – 4

Move a man from the White 12-point to your 8-point.

Move a man from the White 12-point to your 9-point.

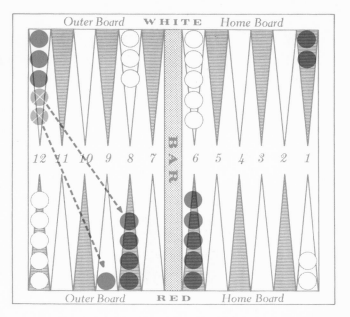

This move is a build-up threat. Your object is to increase the number of follow-up rolls that will make useful points. Your opponent can hit this builder with only six numbers (6–2, 5–3, 4–4, 2–2); if he fails, you have added eight numbers to your key-point-making potential; 6–2 and 2–1 give you the bar-point; 4–3 and 4–1 allow you to make your 5-point. The advantage of eight good throws for you against six good throws for your opponent is sufficient justification for the builder; yet the percentage is even better for two reasons: (a), At least one of the opponent's six "hitting numbers," (2–2), is not likely to be spent hitting a blot, as you will learn in the section on doublet numbers; and (b), even if your follow-up number fails to make a key point, any 4-throw allows you to make the useful 9-point in your outer board while 5–4 or 5–2 on your next throw will enable you to make your 4-point.

However, 5–4 has this drawback: the extra man moved to the 8-point is unlikely to serve an immediate purpose in the battle for points. Nevertheless, the recommended play is superior to using 5–4 strictly as a running number by moving out to White's 10-point with one of your runners.

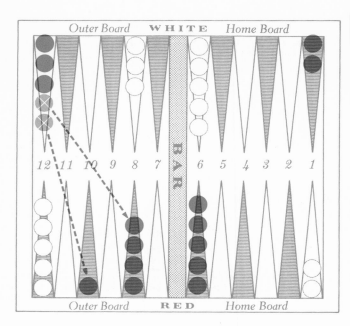

12 11 10 9 8 7 | BAR | 6 5 4 3 2 1

5 – 3

Move a man from the White 12-point to your 8-point.

Move a man from the White 12-point to your 10-point.

1] The 5–3, like the 5–4, follows the flexibility plan by bringing a builder to the 10-point to increase the number of follow-up rolls that will make key points. This is a two-edged builder. White can hit the blot with only five combinations (6–3, 5–4, 3–3): on the other hand, you've only increased your key-point-making potential by six numbers on your next roll. The most useful of these are either 5–3 or 5–1, allowing you to make the 5-point. Another of the added combinations makes the bar-point with 6–3. The other number, 3–1, is not apt to increase your point making potential, since it can be used profitably to make the 5-point, unless your opponent has blocked it via 4–4. (This situation where the same number might be used to gain two different strategic advantages is called *duplication*.)

This evaluation does not even take other good follow-up rolls into account; e.g. 6–2 or 6–4 makes the 4-point. The 5–3 roll suffers from the same basic disadvantage as the 5–4: the man moved to the 8-point does not further your strategic plans. Nevertheless, 5–3 is slightly better than the 5–4, since it creates useful plays for the subsequent 5–3 and the 5–1 which are otherwise undesirable throws.

Until recently, the preferred way to play 5–3 was as a point making number. (See next diagram.)

5 – 3

*Move a man from
your 8-point to
your 3-point.
Move a man from
your 6-point to
your 3-point.*

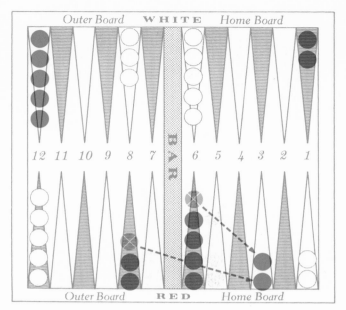

2] Although this play of the 5–3 to make the 3-point used to be preferred, it is slightly inferior to the more flexible build-up threat recommended in the earlier diagram.

Consider what you've learned about points in your home board. The 4-point is good because of its proximity to the 5-point. The 2-point is poor because it fails to blockade the opposing runners and moves two men out of the struggle too early in the game. The 3-point is at best a marginal point in the opening. Until recently, playing the 5–3 in this manner was automatic. However, the value of the build-up threat which makes useful what would otherwise be inferior follow-up throws, such as 5–1, 5–3, 6–3 or even 6–2, has influenced the modern expert to play for potentially useful points rather than settle for the scrawny bird-in-hand.

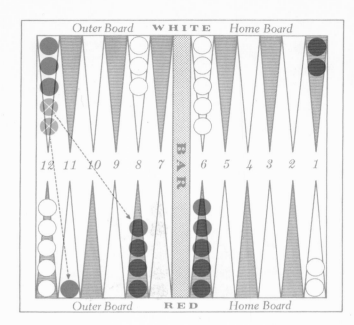

5 – 2

Move a man from the White 12-point to your 8-point.
Move a man from the White 12-point to your 11-point.

1]   As with 5–4 and 5–3, the recommended move, illustrated in this diagram, is designed to increase your flexibility. White can hit the builder on the 11-point with only two throws — 6–4 or 4–6. (Notice that 5–5 does not hit because of your blocking 6-point.) You have increased your point making potential by six throws; 6–4 and 4–1 make the bar-point while 6–3 makes the 5-point. We do not count 6–1, which allows you to make the 5-point, because of "duplication;" 6–1 also makes the bar-point unless White has preempted it with 6–6 — a 35 to 1 shot.

     As in the case with all of the throws in the 5 family, 5–2 suffers from the need to move an extra man to our 8-point.

5 – 2

Play the 5–2 safely by moving a man from the White 12-point to your 6-point as shown.

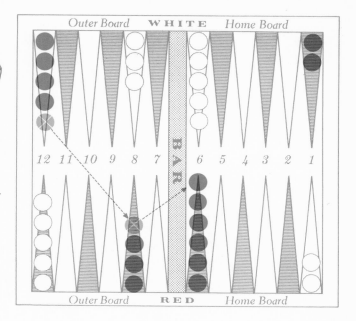

2] (*A beginner's error*) The supposed safety is an illusion; sooner or later you will throw numbers that will force you to leave blots. And blots left early, before the opponent has begun to make up his inner board, are far safer than those you may be compelled to leave later.

In order to win you must make points. A builder on your outer board stands to gain more than it loses; therefore, the "safe" play actually loses ground. If you keep in mind the idea of the advantageous builder, you will never be tempted to make this cowardly play, which reduces the advantage of the first move.

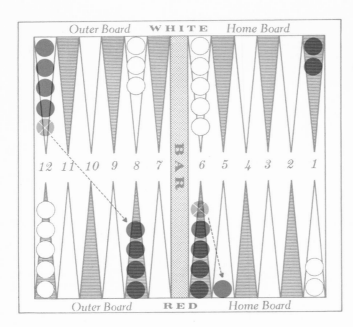

5 – 1

Move a man from the White 12-point to your 8-point.

Move a man from your 6-point to your 5-point.

1] This is a poor throw. One way to try for an advantage is to leave a *direct shot* in your home board. A direct shot is a move which allows your opponent to hit a man with only one die, as opposed to an *indirect shot*, which can only be hit by a combination of two dice. Numbers such as 5–4, 5–3, and 5–2 were moved to your outer board and were reachable only by indirect shots. When a direct shot is offered on your home board in the opening, it is a gambling play.

To justify a blot as a builder, the rule of thumb is the answer to, "DOES IT GAIN MORE THAN IT LOSES?" The same rule is applicable when analyzing a gambling play. White can hit the blot with 15 numbers; all 4s (11 numbers), 3–1, 2–2, and 1–1. In reality, twelve of these rolls are damaging "hits." The 1–1, White will surely play more profitably elsewhere, as will be seen in the "doubles" section. Two more — the 3–1 throws — will cost him the opportunity to make his 5-point if he elects to hit you. If White misses, you can cover the blot, thus making the 5-point with 24 numbers; all 3s and 1s (20 numbers), 6–2, 2–2, and 4–4. Since 14 numbers hit and 24 numbers cover, your potential gain is greater than your potential loss and the gambling play is justified.

However, a placid and quite acceptable alternative is to leave your 6-point intact and split your runners, moving one to White's 2-point. This move does not promise to gain an initiative by making the 5-point, but at the same time, it does not risk the direct shot. If you are unfortunate enough to throw a lot of 5–1s, experiment with both plays.

38

5 – 1

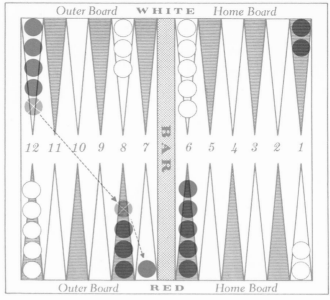

12 11 10 9 8 7 B A R 6 5 4 3 2 1

Outer Board **RED** Home Board

2] Leaving a direct shot on the bar-point instead of the 5-point, as illustrated by this diagram, is inferior. The reason can be found in the concept of gain versus loss. If White fails to hit the bar-point blot, you can cover with 24 numbers — all 6s and 1s (20 throws*), 4–2, 3–3, and 2–2. On the other hand, White can hit the blot with 17 numbers — all 6s (11 numbers), 5–1, 4–2, 3–3, and 2–2. Actually, not all of these "hits" are disastrous; e.g. 6–1 makes his bar-point. For our purposes, the bar-point and the 5-point are approximately equal. In the light of this equality, note the following simple comparison.

	5-point	bar-point
Number of opponent's throws that hit	14	17
Number of your throws that cover	24	24

You have given your opponent three additional hitting numbers and have not increased your covering numbers. Giving an opponent "something for nothing" is good charity but bad backgammon.

* 6–6, 6–5, 6–4, 6–3, 6–1, 1–6, 2–6, 3–6, 4–6, 5–6, 1–1, 2–1, 3–1, 4–1, 5–1, 1–5, 1–4, 1–3, 1–2 (The two 6–1 combinations are counted only once each.)

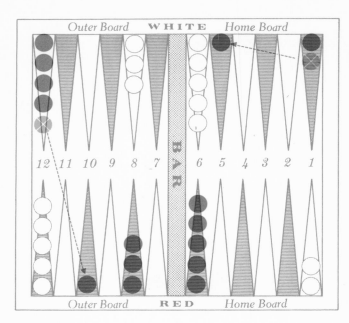

4 – 3

Move a runner to the White 5-point. Move a man from the White 12-point to your 10-point.

1] The interesting move illustrated by this diagram, is our first example of a double purpose first move. The 3 is used to create flexibility by bringing a man to your outer board. The advantages of a builder on the 10-point were analyzed in our discussion of the 5–3. The 4 is an activation move; that is, it mobilizes your runners for aggressive action. The threat of covering his 5-point with your other runner, thus preempting one of your opponent's key points, is a very real one. White may elect to hit this blot on his home board, leaving a blot of his own to prevent your making the 5-point, but doing so exposes him to a great many retaliatory shots. Notice that in this exchange, your risk in the race is very small (five points), while if his blot is hit he would lose twenty.

The dynamic threat of this throw poses White the dilemma of possibly conceding his 5-point or entering upon a dangerous blot-hitting adventure.

The alternate method of moving the 4–3, as illustrated by the next diagram, is playable, though not as strong as the recommended treatment.

4 – 3

Move a man from the White 12-point to your 9-point.

Move a man from the White 12-point to your 10-point.

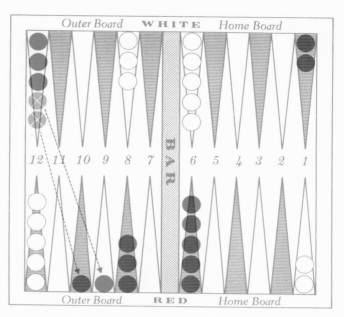

2] This alternate move utilizes the flexibility theme with both men. Obviously both builders can be justified, since each gains more than it loses. White can hit one of your blots with a total of eleven different throws while you have gained fourteen key-point-making throws. The proper play of the 4–3 is the happy choice between two good moves, but the dynamic qualities of the first play makes it the superior choice.

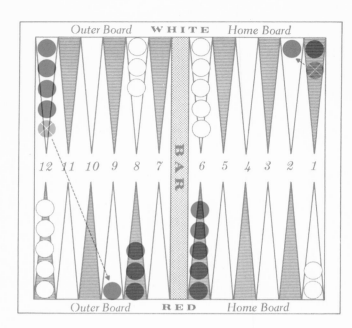

4 – 1

Move a runner from the White 12-point to your 9-point.

Move a runner to the White 2-point.

1] As we have previously discussed the value of a builder on the 9-point, let's concentrate on the modest move which activates your runners. As part of opening strategy, we move builders to the outer board to increase flexibility. We create flexibility in our opponent's home board for the same reason — to increase the number of rolls that are helpful to our game plan. There are two ways in which this type of flexibility is helpful.

The first is a restatement of a familiar idea. What would otherwise be valueless throws can now be used to make useful points. As an example, 4–3 allows you to make White's 5-point, while 6–5 allows you to make White's bar-point.

The second reason is to inhibit White's flexibility by increasing the number of your potential shots. As an example, assume White next rolls 5–2 and plays it in the recommended fashion as shown by the dotted line. If your runners were in their original position, the opposing builder on the 11-point could be hit by only two numbers (6–4). After your 4–1 play, you can hit this builder with six numbers (6–4, 6–3, and 5–4).

This does not mean that White shouldn't play his 5-2 normally. He should and he probably would. It does mean that you've increased his risk in doing so at no cost to your own position.

4 – 1

*Move a man from
the 12-point to
your 9-point.
Move a man from
your 6-point to
your 5-point.*

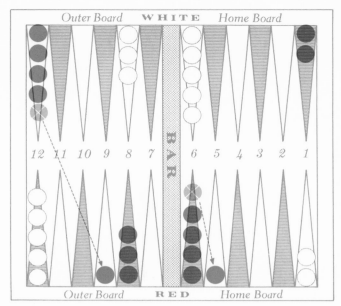

2] This popular alternate play of 4–1 is a gamble. In our analysis of 5–1, we remarked that the blot on the 5-point stands to gain more than it stands to lose. This is the reason why some daring experts make this play, aiming to gain an immediate advantage by making the 5-point.

While recognizing the advantage of the 5-point, our general rule is that if both numbers of your throw can be usefully played, it is not desirable to risk a direct shot. Therefore, this alternate is slightly inferior to the previously recommended play.

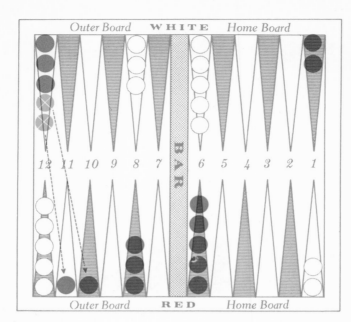

3 – 2
Move a man from the White 12-point to your 11-point.
Move a man from the White 12-point to your 10-point.

1] This aggressive move, as illustrated by the diagram, utilizes the flexibility theme to its utmost. You risk being hit by 6–4, 6–3, 5–4, or 3–3, a total of seven numbers, but in return, you have achieved a great deal of point-making potential. As an example, the bar-point, which could be made only by 6–1 in the original position, can now be made by 4–1, 3–1, 6–4 and 6–3. This method of playing the 3–2 is a sound attempt to gain an early jump on your opponent in the battle for key points.

The next diagram illustrates a less aggressive but fully acceptable alternate move.

44

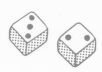

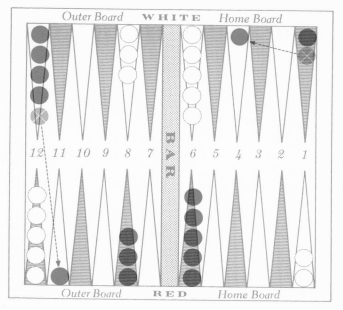

3 – 2

Move a man from the White 12-point to your 11-point.

Move a runner to the White 4-point.

2] With this less aggressive move, you lose the superb flexibility of the previous play but you gain activation of a runner to a good strategic point. This runner acts as a menace against potential White builders in his outer board as we discussed when analyzing the 4–1 move. You also threaten to cover with your other runner, thus making White's 4-point and making it very difficult for him to blockade your runners. You've also gained flexibility of course; 4–1 would make your opponent's 5-point while 6–3 would make his bar-point.

There is little to choose between the two ways of playing 3–2. We advise the reader to try them both and observe the varying positions that develop.

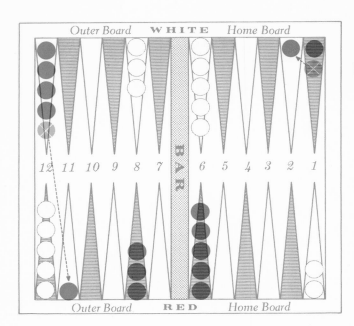

2 – 1
Move a man from the White 12-point to your 11-point.
Move a runner to the White 2-point.

Despite its diminutive size, the 2–1 is a useful throw. The flexibility move to your outer board and the activation of a runner are both progressive moves. A popular alternative is to leave the runners intact and use the 1 as a gambling play by moving a man from the 6-point to the 5-point. While this attempt to make the 5-point is certainly advantageous if you get away with it, we prefer to pose the dual threat rather than risk a direct hit — possibly a double hit if White throws 6–4.

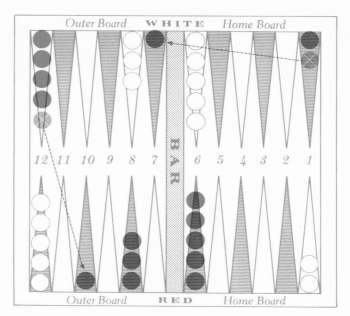

Outer Board **WHITE** Home Board

12 11 10 9 8 7 **BAR** 6 5 4 3 2 1

Outer Board **RED** Home Board

6 – 3

*Move a runner to
the White bar-
point.
Move a man from
the White 12-
point to your 10-
point.*

1] The recommended 6–3 move in this situation employs the tactical theme. The idea behind moving a runner to our opponent's bar-
point is similar to that of the 4–3; White is faced with a dilemma.
Either he allows you to drive a wedge into his position by letting you
make his bar-point or he must hit you, probably leaving a blot exposed to a large number of retaliatory shots. If White elects to hit
your blot, as he is very likely to do, sixteen retaliatory numbers counterhit his exposed man on the bar-point. You are risking very little
in the race as your blot on the bar-point has not moved around the
track any great distance. White's blot on the other hand represents a
potential loss of eighteen points if hit and forced to re-enter on your
home board.

Some of your next throws that do not counterhit are useful in
their own right. As an example, assume that you are hit and your second throw is 5–4. This normally indifferent roll can be profitably
utilized by re-entering on the White 5-point and covering with the
other runner. You are now the proud owner of your opponent's 5-
point.

However, this 6–3 play can lead to difficult problems for the
beginning player. A series of hits and counterhits, or "blot-hitting
contest," can create a complex position that requires the most delicate handling.

Should you prefer to avoid the complications of the tactical
move, try the running move illustrated by the next diagram.

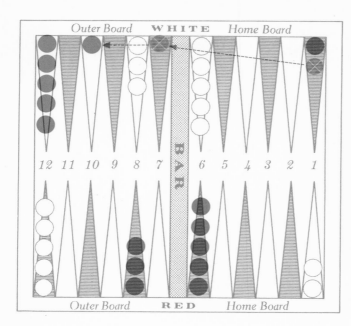

6 – 3

Move a runner to the White bar-point.
Continue with the runner to the White 10-point.

2]   This alternate move, while "standard" for many years, is slowly losing out to the modern expert's preference for the tactical move. To understand why, let's compare the 6–3 as a running number to another running number, 6–4.

As you remember, the 6–4 was vulnerable to only eleven numbers, while the 6–3 can be hit by thirteen numbers; 3s (eleven numbers) and 2–1. One of the justifications for the risk involved in the running 6–4 was that six follow-up numbers would make points in your outer board. There are also six follow-up numbers to make points in your outer board with the 6–3, but two of those numbers, the 4–2, should be used to make the 4-point.

	6–3	6–4
Number of opponent's hits	13	11
Number of outside points	4	6

As this comparison shows that the 6–3 is more likely to be hit and less likely to make outside points than the 6–4, the running play is considered slightly inferior to the tactical play.

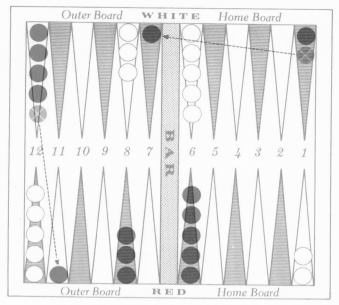

6 – 2

Move a runner to the White bar-point.

Move a man from the White 12-point to your 11-point.

1] This is the second of the tactical plays and the last of the strategic opening moves. White's problems are the same as with the 6–3 in dealing with the Red runner on his bar. Since he would not like you to make his bar-point, he will hit you if possible, even if this exposes him to a potentially unprofitable series of shots and countershots. The key to the tactical play is its forcing quality. Your opponent must alter his normal game plan to deal with direct threats.

The alternate play is to treat the 6–2 as a gambling play as illustrated next.

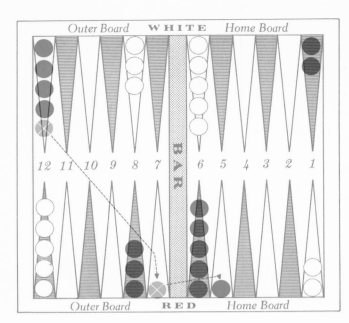

6 – 2

Move a man from White's 12-point to your bar-point. Continue on with the same man to your 5-point.

2] This gambling play stands to gain more than it loses, since twenty-four numbers cover while fourteen numbers hit (the fifteenth throw, 1–1, would not be used to hit). Nevertheless, this is a case of putting all of your eggs in one basket. You have no outside flexibility to fall back on and if White hits your blot, your development will be essentially that of the initial position.

Note the similarity between this position and the position reached after the 5–1 move. Because of this, the gambling play is a less promising alternative to the recommended move.

THE ROLL OF DOUBLETS is not really an opening throw. Except in the rarely played variant in which the first throw of a single die is merely to determine who shall play first, and that player then rolls both dice for his opening move, the first play in the game will always be a non-doublet. However, the roll of doublets will often be the first throw by the other player, and the previously discussed opening moves which frequently apply will no longer serve as a guide.

The doublet roll is unique because it allows you to make four moves instead of the usual two. Most often double numbers are moved in pairs so as to produce new points. As with non-doublets, certain double numbers are better than others. The order of preference is:

1-1, 6-6, 4-4 and 3-3 which are roughly equal, 2-2, then 5-5.

Three of these doublets — 1-1, 6-6, and 5-5 — are usually automatic plays. The other three will vary, depending on the opponent's first play. (For the sake of simplicity, in many cases we have assumed that White's opening throw was 6-5, enabling him to make the Lover's Leap to your 12-point.)

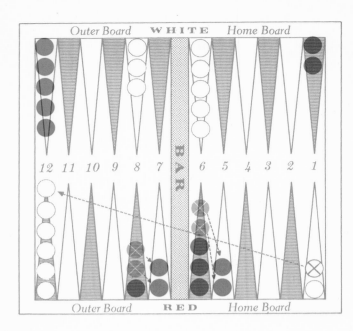

1 – 1

*Move two men
from your 6-point
to your 5-point.
Move two men
from your 8-point
to your bar-point.*

The lowest doublet is also the best doublet. With one move, you have made both of your key points and created quite a problem for White to activate his runners. The indirect shot at your blot on the 8-point should not disturb you since it is in reality a builder for the 4–point.

Future strategy revolves around increasing your blockade. If you can't make the 4-point, try to move a man from the white 12-point to cover the man on your 8-point. You will then have a blockade of four consecutive points and you'll need very little more to establish an overwhelming advantage.

If White had previously activated one of his runners within your home board, the 8-point blot would be subject to a direct hit. Not even this should prevent you from making the recommended play.

Earlier, we indicated that 1–1 would never be used to hit an opponent's gambling play (a blot on the 5-point). It should be clear that the ownership of both your key points is far more valuable.

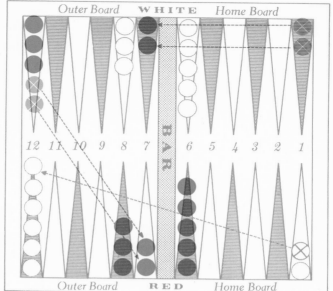

6 – 6

Move two runners to the White bar-point.
Move two men from the White 12-point to your bar-point.

1] This powerful roll not only makes both bar-points, it gives you a good jump in the race. Your future objectives are two-fold; blockading the White runners as usual and trying to move your men off White's bar-point.

The reason you should try to vacate the White bar-point is directly related to the race. If White has not rolled a large double, you are well ahead and his strategy will be to try to contain your former runners. Ideally, the best way to leave his bar would be with doubles since you can safely "travel in pairs."

The reason 6–6 is slightly inferior to 1–1 is a matter of the availability of moves. If White owns either his bar-point or your bar-point, 6–6 does not play well. As an example, consider the following diagram.

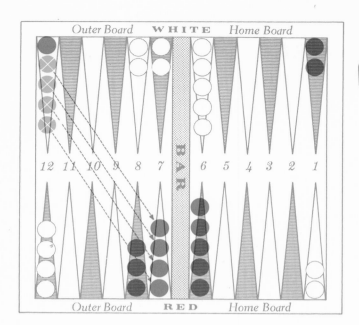

6 – 6

2] Assume that White's first roll was 6–1, making his bar point. You answered by throwing 6–6. With your runners blockaded, the best play as shown by the diagram is to move four men down to your bar point, leaving a shot on the White 12-point. Although this turn of events may displease you, any other move would be worse. (With a key point blocked, a subsequent 1–1 could be handled by making your 5-point and activating your runners.)

54

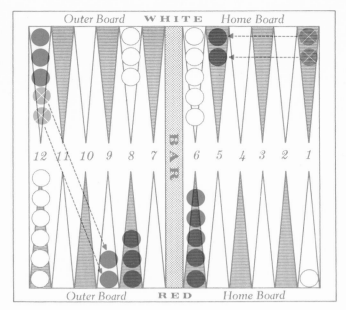

4 – 4

Move your runners to the White 5-point.

Move two men from the White 12-point to your 9-point.

1] While there are alternate ways to play this throw, dependent on the position, the move illustrated is most frequently the appropriate play.

The take-over of White's 5-point frustrates any threat to blockade your runners, and endangers any attempt to bring builders to his outer board.

By making your 9-point, you increase the potential value of your bar-point (four points in a row). You have also created two safe builders for the bar-point and the 5-point. Remember, builders do not need to be blots.

The following diagrams illustrate alternate plays based on specific positional considerations.

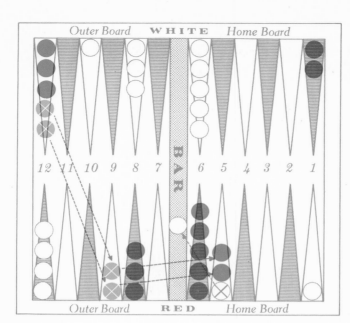

4 – 4
*Move two men
from the White
12-point to your 9-
point.
Continue with the
same two men to
your 5-point.*

2] Let us assume that White gained the first roll with 4–3 and played it in the recommended manner. Since he is threatening to take over your 5-point, your best play is to make the 5-point and at the same time put one of his runners on the bar. This maneuver is known in backgammon argot as "point on his head." While the anatomical reference is in doubt, making the point on White is certainly the correct play.

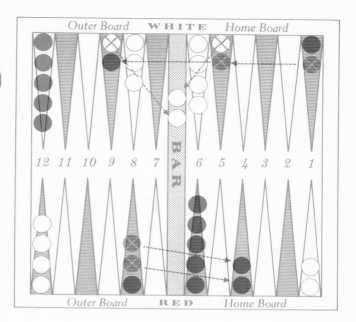

4 – 4

*Move one of your
runners to the
White 5-point.
Continue with
your runner to the
White 9-point.
Move two men
from your 8-point
to your 4-point.*

3]   This is a rare instance where the men are not moved in pairs.
White started with 4–1 and made the gambling move which involved
leaving a blot on his 5-point. Your moves with a runner put both his
blots on the bar. Since he must come in with both men before
beginning to develop his game, making your 4-point creates a very
strong chance that he will not be able to re-enter with both men on
his next throw. If this happens, you will have a winning advantage
at a very early stage in the game.

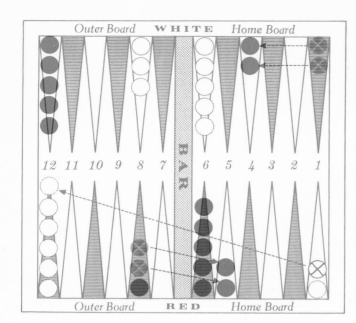

12 11 10 9 8 7 BAR 6 5 4 3 2 1

3 – 3

Move two men from your 8-point to your 5-point. Move both runners to the White 4-point.

Outer Board **R E D** Home Board

1]   The 3–3 is similar to the 4–4 to the extent that the recommended move can be varied depending on the development of the game. Ordinarily, this is the best play since it makes your 5-point and advances your runners, thus frustrating White's attempt to blockade them. Remember, White will be trying to restrict your runners' moves.

Usually, an alternate play is used when it involves hitting a blot. Consider the next diagrams.

58

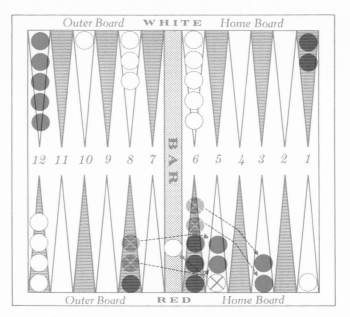

3 – 3

*Move two men
from your 8-point
to your 5-point.
Move two men
from your 6-point
to your 3-point.*

2] White's opening roll was 4–3 which he played in the recommended fashion. You make two points in your inner board, putting his man on the bar and reducing his chances of re-entry.

Notice that there is no urgent need to activate your runners because White is not threatening a blockade at this time. Re-entry will cost him half of his next throw, so there is little danger that he will be able to improve his position significantly.

This move would apply if the White blot were on the 3-point instead of the 5-point. Indeed, some aggressive players make this move even when they don't hit a blot, to mount an early threat against the White runners and against future blots.

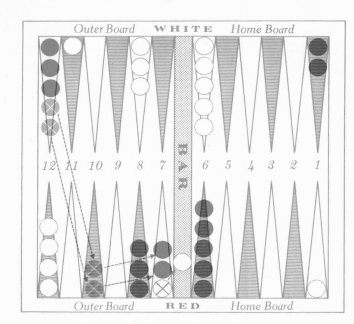

3 – 3
*Move two men
from the White
12-point to your
10-point.
Continue with the
two men to your
bar-point.*

3]   White rolled 6–2 and made the tactical play. His threat to take over your bar-point should be met in the simplest possible way — make the bar-point yourself and simultaneously put his man on the bar.

60

2 – 2

*Move your runners to the White 3-point.
Continue with the runners to the White 5-point.*

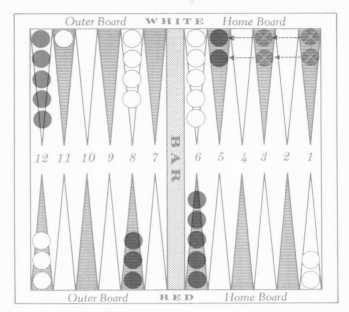

1] This simple play, which occupies White's 5-point, prevents him from setting up any sort of blockade against your runners. Whenever you own an opponent's key point, he will have trouble moving his men into his outer board on the road to home.

As with all double numbers, some enemy deployment has already taken place and White is likely to have started some sort of blockading plan. (In this diagram, we have assumed that he made the approved play for an opening throw of 5–2.)

As a general rule, your runners are best placed on his 5-point where you restrain his movements and at the same time threaten to run out with a future double.

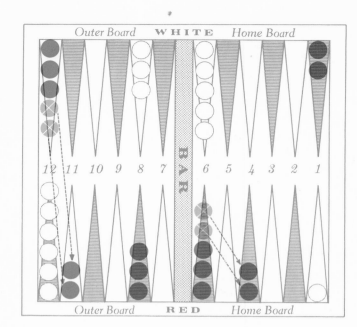

2 — 2

*Move two men
from the White
12-point to your
11-point.
Move two men
from your 6-point
to your 4-point.*

2] This popular alternative should not be employed unless White has not mounted a blockade threat against your runners. The only other time this move is preferable to the White 5-point is when it involves hitting a blot.

5 – 5

Move two men from the White 12-point to your 8-point.

Continue with the two men to your 3-point.

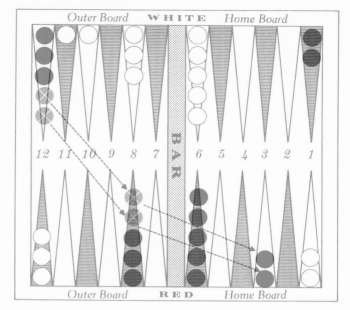

1] When considering the non-doublets, we noted that the "5" family comprised below average rolls. The 5–5 is consistent since it is the poorest doublet. If White has not activated his runners, this is the only acceptable play; in fact, it is close to being the only legal play. If White has activated one of his runners, the alternative play should be made. See next diagram.

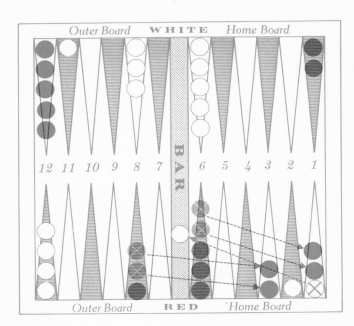

5 – 5

*Move two men
from your 8-point
to your 3-point.
Move two men
from your 6-point
to your 1-point.*

2] We are assuming that White's opening throw of 2–1 was played in the recommended way.

While making the 1 point is not very desirable in the opening, you have closed three points in your home board and placed his runner on the bar. There is some chance that he will not be able to re-enter on the next roll, in which case you've gained an initiative plus an imposing lead in the race. This move should not be made unless a blot is being hit in the process.

Summary of the opening moves

NON DOUBLETS

6 – 5
or
5 – 6

Move a runner to the White 12-point (the Lover's Leap).

6 – 4
or
4 – 6

Move a runner to the White 11-point.

6 – 3
or
3 – 6

Move a runner to the White bar-point.
Move a man from the White 12-point to the Red 10-point.
ALTERNATE:
Move a runner to the White 10-point.

6 – 2
or
2 – 6

Move a runner to the White bar-point.
Move a man from the White 12-point to the Red 11-point.
ALTERNATE:
Move a man from the White 12-point to the Red 5-point.

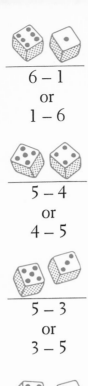

6 – 1
or
1 – 6

Move a man from the White 12-point to the Red bar-point.
Move a man from the Red 8-point to the Red bar-point.

5 – 4
or
4 – 5

Move a man from the White 12-point to the Red 8-point.
Move a man from the White 12-point to the Red 9-point.

5 – 3
or
3 – 5

Move a man from the White 12-point to the Red 8-point.
Move a man from the White 12-point to the Red 10-point.
ALTERNATE:
Move a man from the Red 8-point to the Red 3-point.
Move a man from the Red 6-point to the Red 3-point.

5 – 2
or
2 – 5

Move a man from the White 12-point to the Red 8-point.
Move a man from the White 12-point to the Red 11-point.

5 – 1
or
1 – 5

Move a man from the White 12-point to the Red 8-point.
Move a man from the Red 6-point to the Red 5-point.
ALTERNATE:
Move a man from the White 12-point to the Red 8-point.
Move a runner to the White 2-point.

4 – 3
or
3 – 4

Move a runner to the White 5-point.
Move a man from the White 12-point to the Red 10-point.
ALTERNATE:
Move a man from the White 12-point to the Red 9-point.
Move a man from the White 12-point to the Red 10-point.

4 − 2
or
2 − 4

Move a man from the Red 8-point to the Red 4-point.
Move a man from the Red 6-point to the Red 4-point.

4 − 1
or
1 − 4

Move a man from the White 12-point to the Red 9-point.
Move a runner to the White 2-point.
ALTERNATE:
Move a man from the White 12-point to the Red 9-point.
Move a man from the Red 6-point to the Red 5-point.

3 − 2
or
2 − 3

Move a man from the White 12-point to the Red 10-point.
Move a man from the White 12-point to the Red 11-point.
ALTERNATE:
Move a runner to the White 4-point.
Move a man from the White 12-point to the Red 11-point.

3 − 1
or
1 − 3

Move a man from the Red 8-point to the Red 5-point.
Move a man from the Red 6-point to the Red 5-point.

2 − 1
or
1 − 2

Move a man from the White 12-point to the Red 11-point.
Move a runner to the White 2-point.
ALTERNATE:
Move a man from the White 12-point to the Red 11-point.
Move a man from the Red 6-point to the Red 5-point.

DOUBLETS

6 − 6

Move two runners to the White bar-point.
Move two men from the White 12-point to the Red bar-point.

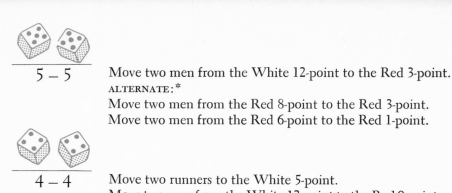

5 – 5   Move two men from the White 12-point to the Red 3-point.
ALTERNATE:*
Move two men from the Red 8-point to the Red 3-point.
Move two men from the Red 6-point to the Red 1-point.

4 – 4   Move two runners to the White 5-point.
Move two men from the White 12-point to the Red 9-point.
ALTERNATE:
Move two men from the White 12-point to the Red 5-point.
ALTERNATE:
Move two men from the Red 8-point to the Red 4-point.
Move two men from the White 12-point to the Red 9-point.

3 – 3   Move two runners to the White 4-point.
Move two men from the Red 8-point to the Red 5-point.
ALTERNATE:
Move two men from the Red 8-point to the Red 5-point.
Move two men from the Red 6-point to the Red 3-point.

2 – 2   Move two runners to the White 5-point.
ALTERNATE:
Move two men from the White 12-point to the Red 11-point.
Move two men from the Red 6-point to the Red 4-point.

1 – 1   Move two men from the Red 8-point to the Red bar-point.
Move two men from the Red 6-point to the Red 5-point.

* This alternate is used when
1] The opposing runners have moved and   2] A blot is hit

III The middle game

IN the previous chapter you learned the opening moves and the reasons they are best. We are now going to consider how to reply to an opening move and how to continue the development of your position.

In each of the following examples your opponent, playing White, has won the opening throw. Once he makes his move, the demands of the position have changed. He may have been lucky enough to make a key point or he may have made a build-up move, a gambling move, a running move or a two-way move. Very often your answering roll is played in the same fashion as you would play an opening throw. Just as often, however, you must play differently because of your opponent's move. Let's consider some of the principles that would affect your decision.

1] WHEN YOUR OPPONENT MAKES A KEY POINT

If White started the game with 3–1, he will make his 5-point. If he started with 6–1 he will make his bar-point. In either case he has achieved an immediate advantage because he is threatening to hem in your runners. Therefore, look for convenient ways to activate and, if possible, to escape with one or both of your runners. As an example, assume that White's opening throw is 3–1, making his 5-point. Let's consider some of your counter moves.

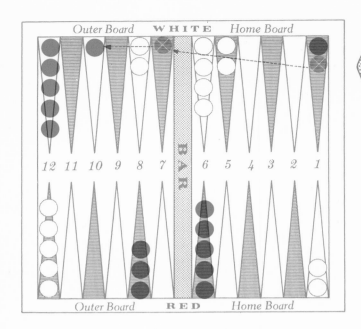

6 – 3: Red's proper play is to run to the White 10-point as shown in the diagram. The logic is simple. Since White is trying to restrain your runners in his home board, get out of his home board as quickly as you can.

In the preceding chapter we recommended the tactical play of moving a runner to White's bar-point and a man to your 10-point. This becomes poor strategy when White owns two points in his home board. From the opening initial position, the odds are 35 to 1 that you can re-enter a man from the bar. When your opponent has two points closed, the odds drop to 8 to 1. While 8 to 1 seems pretty comfortable, failure to re-enter will almost certainly cost you the game. If White hits your man on his bar-point, he will have time to cover this point and have a four-point blockade before you've made any progress at all.

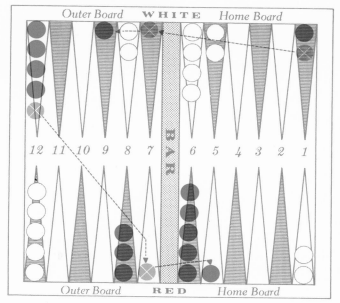

6 – 2:   Try to escape with one of your runners by moving out to the 9-point in an effort to thwart the potential blockade as shown in the diagram.

The tactical opening recommended in the preceding chapter would be poor for the same reason illustrated in our discussion of the 6–3. The gambling play of moving a man from the White 12-point to your 5-point as shown by the dotted line, would be more dangerous because if this blot is hit, the man would be forced to re-enter into an already partially blockaded opposing home board.

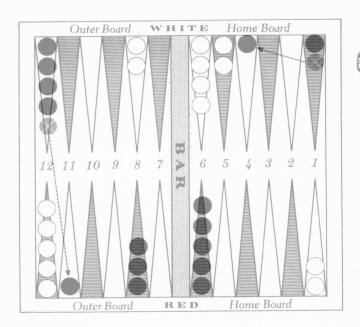

3 – 2:   Bring a runner to the White 4-point. Move a builder to your 11-point.

The reason for activating a runner instead of moving two men to your outer board, as recommended in the preceding chapter, follows the principle of trying to avoid a blockade. You threaten to make your opponent's 4-point which decreases the blockading value of his 5-point. You also make it more dangerous for White to bring a builder to his outer board in an effort to construct his bar-point. If the dice are favorable, on his next throw he will hit your runner on his 4-point in an effort to prevent you from making it. However, this incurs the risk of being counterhit, thus having to come off the bar and start out from your home board.

Notice that if you fail to activate your runner, on his next turn White will be able to bring a builder to his outer board at minimum risk, increasing his chances to construct either his bar-point or his 4-point. If White is allowed to construct his bar-point while you still have two men on his 1-point, his four points in a row will present an imposing blockade.

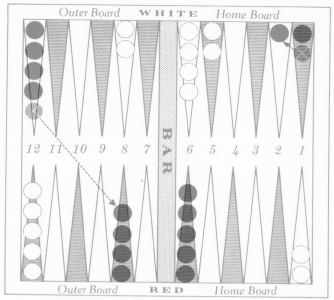

5 – 1: Move a man from his 12-point to your 8-point. Split your runners with the 1.

When we considered this unfortunate opening throw in the previous chapter, we determined that the gambling move which involved bringing a blot to our 5-point was slightly superior to activating the back runners. However, when your opponent has the 5-point, it becomes imperative that you do activate the back runners as illustrated by the diagram. This doubles the number of indirect shots with which you can hit a potential builder brought to White's outer board; at the same time, it prepares for follow-up numbers that will allow you to advance your runners. For example, on your next roll, 3–2 will make his 4-point and 6–5 will make his bar-point.

This same principle of activating a runner with the 1 and bringing down a builder applies to 4–1 and 2–1. (6–1 and 3–1 are, of course, used to make our bar-point and our 5-point respectively).

When the opponent has made a key point on his opening roll and your follow-up throw offers alternate treatments, choose the one which activates your runners, thus trying to reduce the effectiveness of his potential blockade. Avoid tactical plays or gambling plays, which become more dangerous as the chances of immediate re-entry of a man on the bar are lessened by your opponent's occupation of additional points in his inner board.

Your strategy in this case can be summed up in one sentence. Try to hit his builder with one of your runners unless your throw is a doublet that can be played more profitably elsewhere. As an example, consider the position of the following diagram.

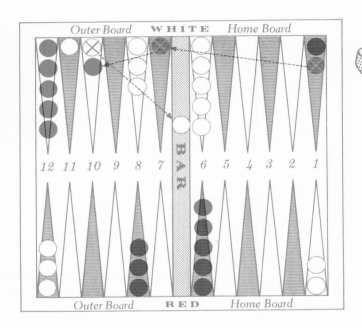

6 − 3 or 5 − 4: Hit the opposing blot on White's 10-point. Your answer to White's opening 3–2 is 6–3 or 5–4. The treatment recommended when 6–3 or 5–4 is the first throw in the game would not be as profitable as using one of your runners to hit White's blot on the 10-point.

You should not hit the blot if you roll 3–3. This doublet can be used more profitably to make your 5-point and bring your two runners to the White 4-point.

In general, always employ a non-doublet to hit an opposing builder in your opponent's outer board. With doublets, you may or may not hit his builder.

In the previous example we did not hit the builder with 3–3. On the other hand, consider the next diagram.

74

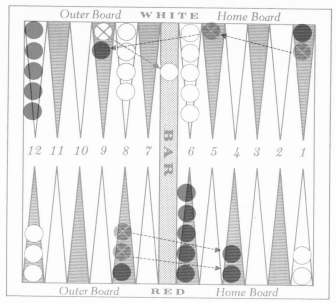

4–4: Move one runner to hit the blot on White's 9-point. Move two men from your 8-point to make your 4-point.

White's opening throw was 5–4. If your counter roll were 5–3 or 6–2, you would of course hit the blot. (*A non-doublet should be used to hit a blot in your opponent's outer board.*)

Two doublets, 4–4 and 2–2, are within range of your opponent's builder. 4–4 should be used partly to hit by moving a runner to the White 9-point, and partly to construct your own 4-point as shown by the dotted line. You have achieved three excellent aims: activated one of your runners; made a strategically sound point in your own home board; and placed an opponent's man on the bar.

However, the other doublet, 2–2, should not be used to hit the blot. Either making White's 5-point or making your own 11-point and your 4-point would be preferable.

A third possibility — making White's 3-point and your own 4-point — should be rejected as a halfway measure. Holding White's 5-point is both a forward-going play and a serious threat against any builders White may wish to bring into his outer board. If you elect to make the 4-point in your home board, posting two men on your 11-point will have greater potential value as blockers and builders than the puny extra worth of advancing your runners from the 1-point to the 3-point.

A doublet should be used to hit a blot in your opponent's outer board only when part of that doublet can be used to make an effective point in your home board.

3] *WHEN YOUR OPPONENT MAKES A GAMBLING PLAY*

As you remember, a gambling play involves leaving a blot on the 5-point in the hopes of making that point on the next throw. If your opponent has done this, *hit the blot whenever you can.* The only exception comes if you roll 1–1, because that number allows you to make both your bar-point and your 5-point. No hit is worth foregoing such an advantage.

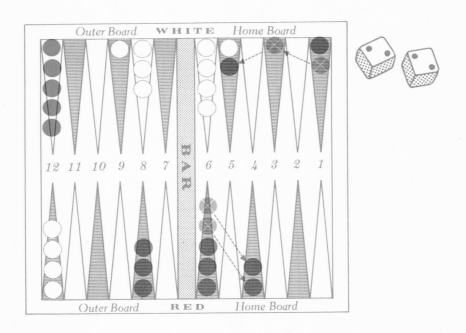

2 – 2: Hit the blot on White's 5-point with one runner. Make your 4-point by moving two men from the 6-point.

White elected to make the gambling play with his opening roll of 4–1. Any counter throw with a 4 on one of your dice should be used to hit the blot on his 5-point. If your roll is 2–2, the proper treatment is to make your 4-point and to hit the blot with a runner as shown in the diagram.

Suppose instead of 2–2 you rolled 3–1. It is very tempting to

76

make your 5-point and indeed, that would not be a bad play. However, it is better to hit the blot for the following reason. If you make your 5-point and on the next throw your opponent makes his 5-point (which he is very likely to do), you have achieved nothing but equality. If, on the other hand, you hit the blot, you have put a man on the bar, assuring yourself of at least a temporary advantage.

4] WHEN YOUR OPPONENT MAKES A TACTICAL PLAY

The tactical play can lead to what is known as a "blot-hitting contest." Your bar-point can become an area of hit and counterhit, and during the course of this, you may need to re-enter several of your men on your opponent's home board. Don't be afraid. Hit him on your bar-point if you can. Examine the following short blot-hitting contest illustrated in the following diagrams.

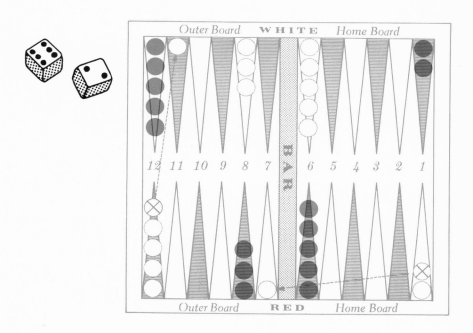

6 – 2: White plays his opening roll in the recommended fashion by moving a runner to your bar-point and bringing a builder to his 11-point.

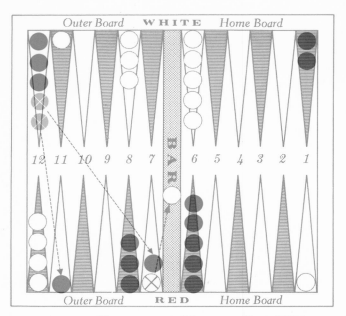

6 – 2: You are unwilling to allow White to "take over" your bar-point. You use your 6–2 to hit the White runner and bring a builder to your 11-point.

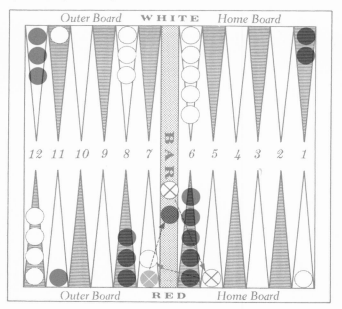

5 – 2: White strikes back by re-entering his man from the bar and continuing to hit your man on the bar-point. He has the temporary advantage of forcing you to lose ground in the race.

78

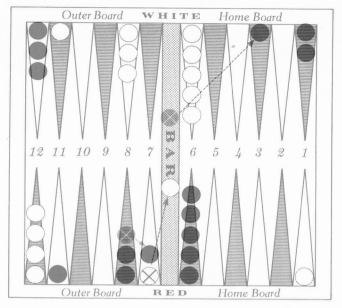

3 – 1:   You use this throw to continue the same game plan, re-entering your blot on the White home board with the 3 and hitting the opponent's man on your bar-point with the 1.

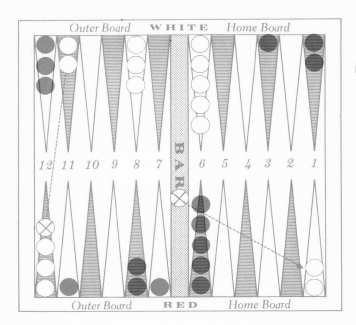

2 – 1: This throw ends the blot-hitting contest abruptly. White has nothing better than to re-enter his man with the 1 and cover his builder on the 11-point with the 2.

Notice that you are now an overwhelming favorite to make your bar-point on the next throw. In fact, 29 numbers will make the bar-point, while only 7 numbers miss. The prospect of acquiring this excellent blockading point is more important than the ground lost in the race, and you should be quite content with the outcome.

Do not be misled by how quickly and favorably this blot-hitting contest ended. Sometimes, if it continues for many moves, you may end up with five or six men in your opponent's home board, hopefully making at least two points there. This is far from a desperate state of affairs, however. It will be very difficult for your opponent to bring his men around the board without leaving a number of blots. In the interim you will have a chance to construct valuable points in your home board, thus increasing his re-entry problems when and if you finally hit him. The back game described in Chapter x will illustrate this very point. Until then, the one message we are trying to deliver is: DON'T HESITATE TO COMPETE FOR YOUR OWN BAR-POINT.

The following four diagrams are informal quizzes. Try to work out the correct moves and the reasons behind them before looking at the answers.

In response to your opponent's opening 6–2, you roll 3–3. What is the best way to play this doublet and why?

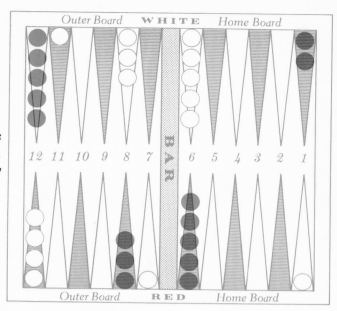

ANSWER: Use the 3–3 to make your bar-point and put White's runner on the bar. White has offered to engage you in a blot-hitting contest with his opening move. You've gained a tremendous advantage in your ensuing roll!

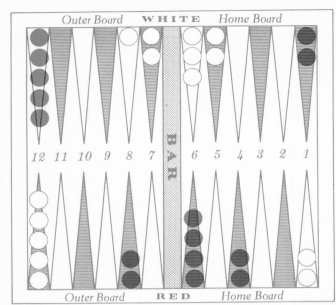

You won the opening roll with 4–2 and made your 4-point. Your opponent responded with 1–1 (the best number on the dice), making both key points. Your next roll is 5–2. How do you play this number and why?

ANSWER: 5–2 is normally a bad early roll, but in this case it serves a good purpose: you can hit the exposed man on White's 8-point with one of your runners. The usual opening play (bringing a man to your 8-point and a man to your 11-point) would give White a chance to cover his blot on the 8-point or to make his 4-point, either of which would give him a blocking position of four consecutive points against your runners.

82

In comparison to your opponent's bar-point and outer board builders, you have not accomplished very much with your opening throw of 2–1. Your next roll is 4–3. How do you play this number and why?

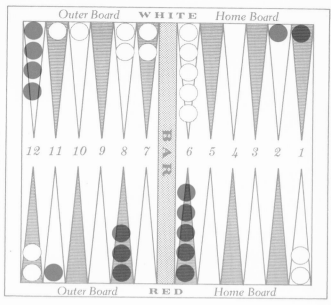

ANSWER: Following best procedure, you have activated your runners against White's partial blockade. Now you can use this activation to good purpose by making your opponent's 5-point, thus reducing the effectiveness of his bar-point.

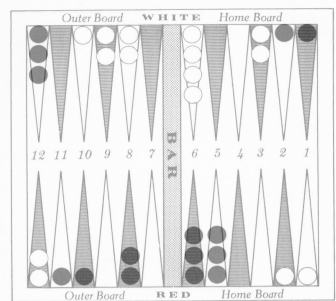

There are three seemingly attractive ways to play your 4–3.

a] *Make your opponent's 5-point.*

b] *Make your own bar-point.*

c] *Make your 2-point and simultaneously put your opponent's runner on the bar.*

You would like to be able to play this number three times; however, the rules do not permit this. So, rank the three plays in order of preference, remembering what you've learned about blockading, being blockaded, and the key points.

ANSWER: If you answered this one correctly, you have already gained considerable insight into backgammon theory. The best play is to make your bar-point. You will have four points in a row, blockading the White runners, with two builders in position (on the 6-point and on the 5-point) threatening to make the 4-point and construct a five-point blockade, the nearest thing to a prime.

Making your opponent's 5-point is certainly a good play, but slightly inferior to making your bar-point. White has loads of potential but your split runners are in no trouble unless he can make his 5-point fast. (Since it's very likely he will be able to do this within the next roll or two, your next order of business will be to try to advance your runners. Having made your bar-point, if you can manage to escape cleanly with at least one runner, your position will be overwhelming.)

Making your 2-point and hitting the blot, while tempting, is the poorest of the three alternatives. Earlier, discussing the opening roll of 6–4, we determined that making the 2-point is unimportant. The 2-point is somewhat more tempting here, because it hits a blot and makes a third point in your inner board. Nevertheless, it is a mistake to sacrifice position at this early stage of the game.

5] *WHEN YOUR OPPONENT MAKES A RUNNING PLAY*

Hit any blot in your outer board, except when you can make either your bar-point or your 5-point. Logically, since he is trying to escape with a runner, you should stop him if you can. The only problem arises if your counter roll is a similar running move. Examine the position illustrated by the diagram.

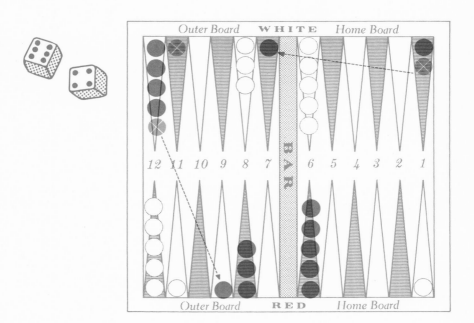

White opened with 6–4, bringing a runner out to your 11-point. Your counter roll is also 6–4. It would be incorrect for you to make the same play as White, because you choose a running play only if the odds are that you will not be hit. If you run to the White 11-point (as shown by the "✕") White's man on your 11-point makes him a favorite to hit you. (Twenty numbers hit, sixteen numbers miss.) Therefore, you should choose to use the 6–4 as a tactical play, moving a runner to your opponent's bar-point and a man to your

85

9-point. In some ways this is actually better than the same tactical play as your opening move. If White hits your blot on the bar-point, you have the possibility of an additional target for retaliation — White's blot on your 11-point.

As a general principle: When you roll a running number in response to your opponent's running number, if you can't hit him, make a tactical play.

The main message of this chapter is simply this: As the position changes, different throws should be used for different purposes. Ask yourself after each throw of the dice:

a] Should I hit an opponent's blot? Should I be trying to make points? Should I be trying to mobilize my runners? Or should I move builders into position?

b] How does the immediate throw affect my aims?

In the next chapter, you will learn the proper technique to maximize your chances of winning in the stretch run.

iv Bringing home your men

ONCE you have brought all of your men as far as your outer board and are no longer concerned with threading your way through the advanced blocking points owned by your opponent, your objective is to get your men into your home board so you can start bearing off.

If your opponent still has men in your home board or on the bar and has not yet had to break up his own home board, your principal consideration must be safety, so as to maintain your lead in the race. This may involve future safety, as well as immediate safety. In some situations, you will be better off leaving a single combination shot — that is a blot that can be hit by only one specific roll — rather than getting into a position where you are in danger of leaving one or more direct shots in the near future.

But if contact no longer exists — your opponent's men having also broken into the clear — your moves will be dictated by two considerations:

First: Economy, i.e., getting all your men into your home board as soon as possible, so that you can begin to bear off.

Second: Diversification, i.e., placing men on as many different points as possible so that you will increase your chance of bearing off a man with *each* of the two numbers of your future throws.

The following diagram involves the application of both these principles.

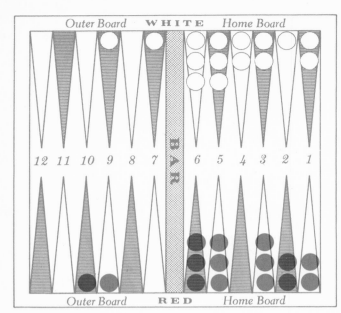

In this neck and neck race, you (Red) throw 5–2. Do you use the 5 to move a man from your 10-point, 9-point, or 6-point? How do you play the 2?

The 2 cannot bring either man home, so let's first consider the 5. You should use it to bring the man on your 9-point to your 4-point. Economy, since it brings a man home, plus diversification, since it places a man on your vacant 4-point.

Suppose instead, you moved the man from your 10-point to your 5-point and your next throw leaves the 4-point unoccupied. As long as you have men on your 6-point and 5-point, every time you throw a 4, you will lose the opportunity to bear a man off; you cannot legally waste a single pip of your throw so you must advance a man from one of those higher points.

It should now be obvious that the worst play for the 5 would be to move a man from your 6-point. It does nothing to facilitate moving your men home (economy), nor does it serve the purpose of diversification.

How to use the 2 is a tossup. Some experts will advance the man on the 10-point closer to your home board; others will move another man from the 6-point to the 4-point. We lean towards this latter choice to further diversify, or "smooth out," your home board position. Only if your next throw is 2–1 will you be unable to bear a man off.

When the preferred move in a non-contact racing situation seems to be a tossup, the conflict can be settled in some cases by the use of the *crossover principle* (see diagram).

88

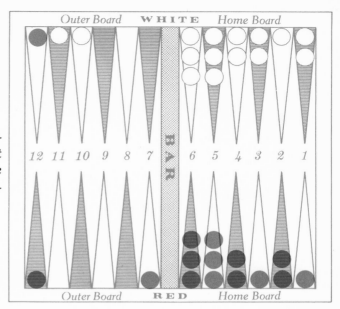

You are Red in this non-contact race and have just thrown a 5–4. What is the proper way to play this number?

The 4 is easy enough. You move the man on your bar-point to the 3-point, thus smoothing out your home board (diversification) and bringing a man on your outer board into your home board (economy).

The 5 is more difficult. You must choose which of your two remaining outside men to move, since your prime objective at this time is to bring all of your men home so that you can begin bearing off. Neither play brings a man home and neither play aids diversification. It is here that the *crossover principle* comes into play: *move the man that can be brought forward into the next table.*

In this example, you bring your man from the 12-point to your 8-point. Note the effect: on your next throw, you will be able to bring *both* men home with 6–5, 6–4, 6–3, 6–2 and 2–2 — nine chances that would not be present if you had previously elected to use the 5 to bring your man from your 12-point to your bar-point.

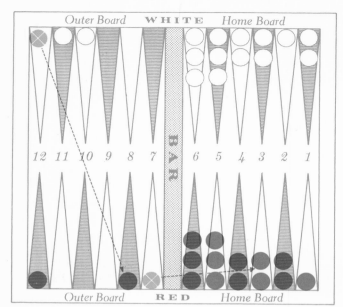

Here you move the man from the White 12-point to your 8-point, *crossing from White's outer board to your outer board.* If, on your next throw, a 6 appears on either die, any number but a 1 on the other die allows you to bring both of your last two men home. You will then be ready to use both dice on your next throw to begin bearing off. In other words, a moderately lucky throw allows you to get home with one roll as opposed to one and-one-half rolls, which would be necessary without a crossover. Try moving the 5 from the Red 12-point and you will realize that, on your next turn, no non-doublet will bring both outside men home.

The crossover principle can be vital in certain positions. Consider the following unfortunate situation.

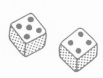

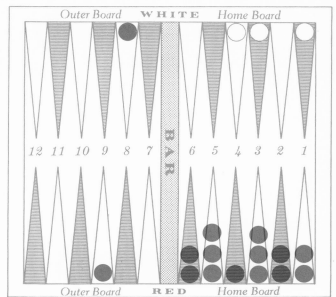

You (Red) are struggling to avoid losing a gammon. You are trying to remove a man before White removes all of his men. You have just thrown 5–4. Assuming that White will not throw an appropriate doublet, what is your best chance to save the gammon?

Diversification has become meaningless since you aren't going to win. Your only object is to remove a man; thus economy, plus the crossover principle, will help to determine the proper move. The correct play is to move the man on your 9-point to your 5-point (economy) and move your man on the White 8-point to the Red 12-point. On your next throw you will have fifteen chances out of thirty-six to save the gammon (eleven 6s, 2–2, 3–3, 4–4 and 5–5).

If you make the incorrect play of moving the man on your 9-point to your 4-point and your man on the White 8-point to the White 12-point, only four chances out of thirty-six can save the gammon for you, (3–3, 4–4, 5–5 and 6–6). Even the obviously unsound play of taking the 5–4 by bringing your back man to your 8-point and leaving two men outside your home board would actually be better, adding the chance that you could get a man off with 2–2.

In the following chapter we will further discuss the problems of the straight race and finally of removing your men from the board.

v Bearing off: the stretch run

AS SOON as your last man is inside your home board you are ready to begin bearing off. Your *moves* are governed first of all by the exact number of pips on each die you cast. Your strategy is governed by whether or not you are still in a contact game. If any risk of being hit remains, your primary consideration is safety. If you are in a straight race, your twin objectives are economy and diversification.

Let's briefly review the laws that control this part of the game:

1] All fifteen men must be in your home board before you begin to bear off.

2] Bearing off is done strictly according to the number on each die; e.g. if you roll a 5–2, you may remove a man from the 5-point and a man from the 2-point if men are on those points, but:

3] You must use as much of your throw as possible; e.g. if you throw a 5 on one die and have no men on the 6-point or 5-point, you may bear off a man from the 4-point. If, on the other hand, you have no men on the 5-point but a man on the 6-point, you *must* use this 5 to move your man from the 6-point to the 1-point.

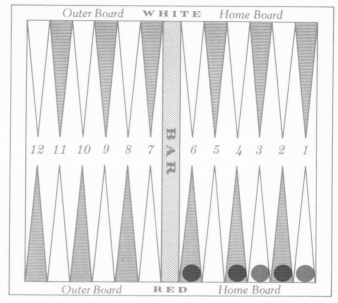

Exception: *You may play the numbers on your dice in any order you choose.* Suppose you throw 5–2 in the diagrammed position where you have one man on each point except your 5-point. You need not play the 5 from your 6-point to your 1-point; then remove a man from your 2-point. You may play the 2 to advance a man to your 4-point; then take a man off the 4-point by using the 5. The advantage is that you will remain with a man on your 2-point and will not fail to bear a man off if you throw a 2 on your next roll.

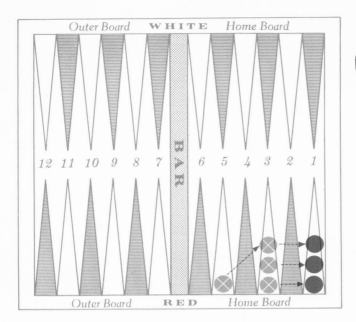

4] Doublets are, as usual, played twice. Thus, if you roll 2–2 and have four men on your 2-point, you may bear off four men. But if you have no man on an even numbered point you may have to advance men from your 5- and 3-points, and fail to bear off a single man as shown in the diagram, even though only three of your men remain on the board.

NON-CONTACT TACTICS

In a straight race you can usually determine whether or not you are ahead by counting "pips;" i.e. by determining the minimum total you must throw in order to bring the last man off. Each pip on a die is equivalent to one space on the board.

For the sake of simplicity, we'll start from the ending of a game in the following diagram, and work our way back to the less easily calculated positions where more men are still in play.

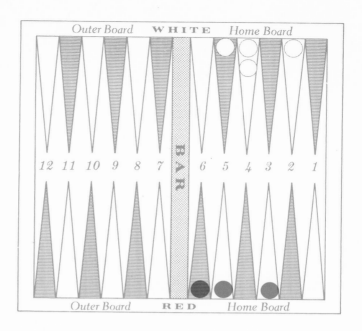

You need to take off only three men to win the game; white, your opponent, must bear off four. To remove your man from the 6-point, you must total six pips on your dice. A total of five pips would bring that man only to the 1-point. Similarly, the man on the 5-point requires at least five pips to bear it off while the man on the 3-point requires at least three pips. If we add these together, we get a total of 14 pips which means that your successive rolls of the dice must total at least 14 to bear off all of your men. Now consider White's position. One man on the 5-point equals five pips: two men on the 4-point equal eight pips (four pips × two men): his man on the 2-point adds two pips, for a total of fifteen pips. This position is very even and the player whose turn it is to throw has an apparent advantage. (Since this discussion involves only pip-counting, let us for the moment disregard the fact that with only three men in play you can afford one miss, while White cannot afford any. Ignoring doublets, White will lose if he throws a 1 on either cast, a 3 on his first cast or a 2 on each of two casts. Red is a favorite to win unless he fails to throw a 6, 5, or 3 on his first roll.)

The counting of pips is simply a determination of how many points have to be traversed before removing all of the men from the board.

Now let's count out a position where both sides are about to begin bearing off. The fact that White still has one man left on his bar-point is trivial since on his next roll, he will bring the man home with one die and remove a man from the board with the other die. Before reading the analysis of this diagram, try to count the pips yourself and decide if you, Red, are ahead or behind in the race.

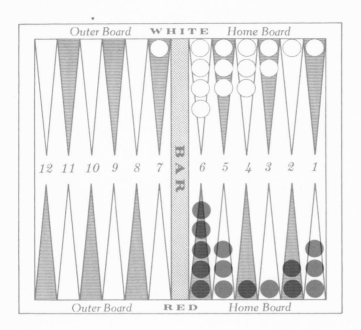

One way to count the pips for each side is to multiply each point's number by the number of men that are on it. Applying this to the diagram, we get:

RED POSITION					WHITE POSITION			
Point		*Men*		*Pips*	*Point*		*Men*		*Pips*
6	×	5	=	30	7	×	1	=	7
5	×	3	=	15	6	×	4	=	24
4	×	1	=	4	5	×	3	=	15
3	×	1	=	3	4	×	3	=	12
2	×	2	=	4	3	×	2	=	6
1	×	3	=	3	2	×	1	=	2
					1	×	1	=	1
				59 pips					67 pips

We have a healthy, though not insurmountable, lead of eight pips in the race. What do these eight pips mean? The average number expectancy for each cast of two dice is a little more than eight pips, which means that you are ahead by almost a full roll. Being able to determine precisely how far ahead or behind you are at any stage of a non-contact game will become critically important in the next chapter which deals with when to double and when to accept an opponent's double. In general, in a non-contact bear-off: *If you are approximately equal or ahead in the race, diversify your men as much as possible to take advantage of as many numbers as you can. If you are approximately a roll or more behind in the race, move your men so as to be able to take maximum advantage of hoped-for doublets, since you'll need lucky throws to win the game.* To illustrate this principal, examine this position:

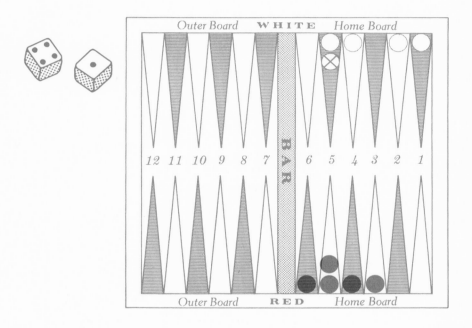

4–1: After taking a man off your 4-point, you must make a decision on how to play the 1. This decision is directly dependent upon how you stand in relation to your opponent. A pip count tells you that after you play the 4–1, you will be 18 pips away from winning while your opponent has 17 pips to go. In this close race, you should move a man from your 5-point to your 4-point, thus *diversifying your men* in an effort to take maximum advantage of your next throw. Now assume that White's man marked with an "x" is not on the board. A pip count would tell you that after taking your 4–1, you are seven pips, or almost a full roll, behind in the race. A further examination tells you that there is a good chance that he will bring off all of his men in two throws. Your next throw is likely to be your last of the game. If you make the diversification play, the only roll that will take all four men off is 6–6. You should therefore move your 1 from the 6-point to the 5-point. Now 6–6 or 5–5 will win the game. You're likely to lose the game anyway, but you've doubled your chances for a miracle.

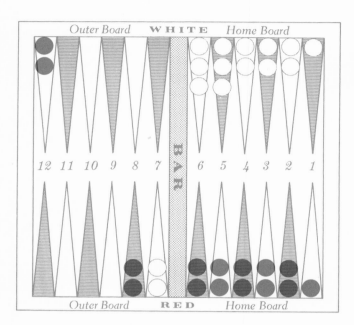

Here's a position from the late middle game to show how pip counting can dictate a crucial play.

In this situation it is difficult to bring your men home from the White 12-point without leaving a shot to the opponent's men on your bar-point. White is, of course, having the same difficulty leaving your bar-point without leaving a shot. It is your throw and you roll 3–3. Should you move the men on your 8-point six points each and play for a shot or should you move the men from the White 12-point to your 10-point in an effort to convert the game to a non-contact race? The answer can be readily determined by counting pips. Before you play the 3–3, White's pip count is 88, while your pip count is 82. This means that before your throw, you were ahead by six pips. Add the twelve pips you've gained by rolling 3–3, and you find that you are 18 pips ahead in the race. Obviously you should run off the White

12-point, trying to convert the game from a holding position to a non-contact race.

In an equal position, the principal of diversification is very important. Lack of diversification can lead to a game where a player ahead on pips is hopelessly lost in the race. Determine how you stand in the race in the following position.

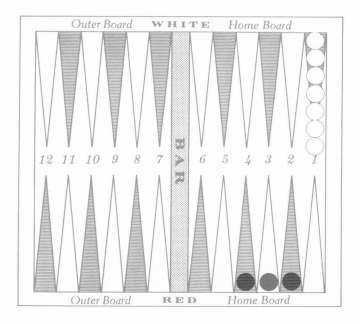

On a pip count, White is two pips ahead of you, 7 to 9 pips, yet White has a close-to-hopeless race. Assuming that neither side throws a doublet, you are very likely to bear off all of your men within two rolls; White needs four. Is this a paradox? Not really. Every time White rolls the dice, he is wasting pippage since any throw will take off two men; e.g. if he throws 6–5, it has the same bear-off value as 2–1. The advantage of diversification lets you use your throws to maximum advantage.

Another consideration is the number of men you have left on the board. In this case, White must bear off seven men to win, while you need to bear off only three. Does this mean that counting pips is not valuable in the final stages of the game? Absolutely not. The technique of counting pips provides you with a very accurate pair of spectacles. But spectacles are not substitutes for eyes.

In summary, the relative potential of the two armies must take into account:

1] The pip count.
2] Degree of diversification.
3] The number of men each side still has on the board (specific number of rolls required).

BEARING OFF IN CONTACT

While an opponent maintains contact, the process of diversification and swift removal of your men must give way to consideration of safety. The position may be the result of success in trapping his runners or it may be due to your opponent's blocking strategy. The most usual, as well as the most valuable, point for your opponent to hold is your 1-point, known in backgammon parlance as an *ace-point game*. Let's look at Red's problems in this situation.

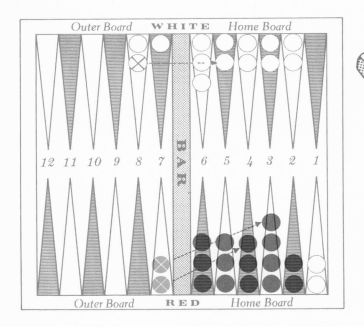

In this game, White's runners were trapped behind a prime. Since his home board is well prepared for visitors, you must be as careful as possible not to leave a shot. There is no question of counting pips in this type of a game; you are far ahead in the race, and may even gammon your opponent, provided he is unable to hit a blot. It is your roll. Notice that there is immediate jeopardy. If you throw a 6–5, you have no legal 6 and your only 5 is from your bar-point to your 2-point, leaving a blot on your bar-point. If White is able to hit that blot, he will probably win the game because of your re-entry problems. Luckily, your throw is 4–3, and you are able to clear the bar-point as shown by the dotted lines. You are now ready to begin bearing off.

White throws a 2–1 which he uses to bring a man to his 5-point as shown by the dotted line. The 2–1 is a good throw for White because he has no chance in the race and would like to keep his home board intact in the event he gets a shot.

You now throw 6–6, and in accordance with the rules, remove the three men from the 6-point and one man from the 5-point to arrive at the position shown.

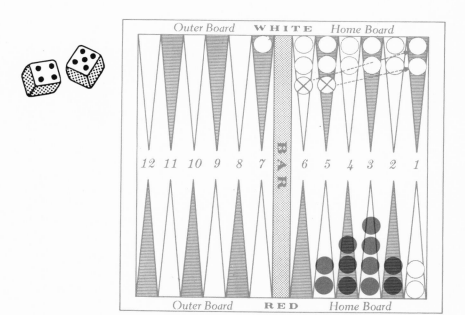

White throws a 5–4 and moves a man from his 6-point and a man from his 5-point to his 1-point, closing his home board. It is your throw. If you roll 6–6, 5–5, 6–4, 5–4 or 4–2, a total of ten throws, there is no way to avoid leaving a blot. Please convince yourself of this by experimentation. The number you *do* throw is 4–4 and you remove the three men from the 4-point. Notice that there is no legal way to play a fourth 4 since the men on your 5-point are

101

blocked, so you must forego this much of your roll. (If you had no men on the 5-point, you would, of course, remove a man from the 3-point.) White throws a 2–1 and moves his man from his bar-point to his 4-point to arrive at this new position.

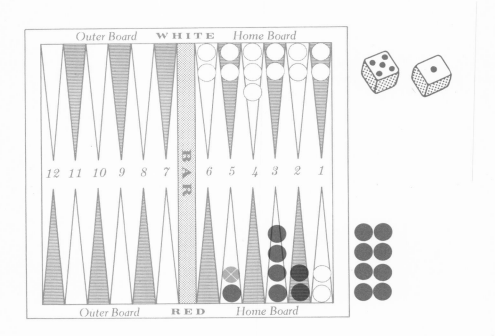

Although you have not yet left a shot, the dice did not permit you to bear off in the safest fashion. There is a gap between the 5-point and the 3-point which is a trouble potential. There are, in fact, fourteen bad throws for you in this position: 6–4, 6–1, 5–4, 5–1, 4–3, 4–2 and 4–1 all leave blots. Ideally, the best way to bear off is to clear the points on your home board in descending order; that is, clear the 6-point, followed by the 5-point, followed by the 4-point, and so on.

It is your throw, and this time your luck does not hold; you throw a 5–1. Since you are compelled to remove a man from the 5-point, as shown by the "x," the only question is how to play the 1. Your two choices are either to move a man from your 3-point to your 2-point or to move your blot from the 5-point to the 4-point. Only an inexperienced player will "guess" whether White will roll a three or a four at his next turn; there is only one right play. Can you tell which one and why?

If White hits your blot, the game is up for grabs. You do, of course, have eight men already borne off and if you are hit, you may be able to re-enter quickly while White is bearing off, scoot around the board and win the race by a hair, but you'd rather not have to try to do this. Your first concern is to leave White the slimmest possible chance to hit. If you leave the blot on the 5-point, he can hit you with thirteen numbers — eleven 4s and 3–1. If you move your blot to the 4-point, he can hit you with eleven 3s. Therefore, you play the percentages and give your opponent two fewer chances by moving the blot to the 4-point. *Whenever you have to leave a shot in a contact bear-off, try to minimize your opponent's potential hits.*

We will leave this position since whether or not White hits the blot is a matter of luck and you can be content that you made the most of the numbers you threw.

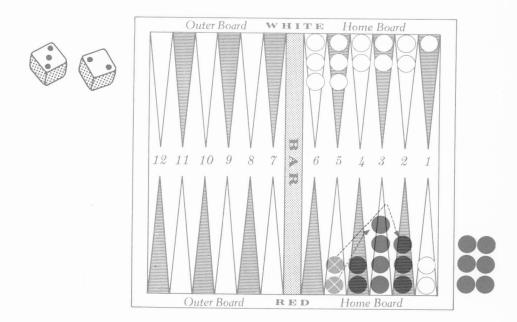

In the previous positions, most of your moves were controlled by the vagaries of the dice. In the position of this diagram, you will have something to say about how to take your moves.

Having already borne off six men, you have just thrown 3-2. Keeping in mind that there is no question of losing the race, the proper play is to clear your 5-point as shown by the dotted line. If you use the 3 to take a man off the 3-point, any 2 you move leaves a blot.

103

After White throws a 4–1 and closes his board, by moving a man from his 5-point to his 1-point, you roll 6–2. A man on the 4-point, must be borne off the board. What is the correct way to play the 2? If you remove a man from the 2-point, you are leaving an unnecessary blot. The correct play, of course, is to clear the 4-point by moving the blot to the 2-point. Remember, you are not required to bear a man off if there is an alternate legal play.

The same principles apply when your opponent owns some point in your home board other than the 1-point. The only difference is that once you've borne off the men on the points *in front* of the blocker, your style shifts to that of a non-contact game. The more advanced the blocker's point, the less effective is its threat. To illustrate, consider this position.

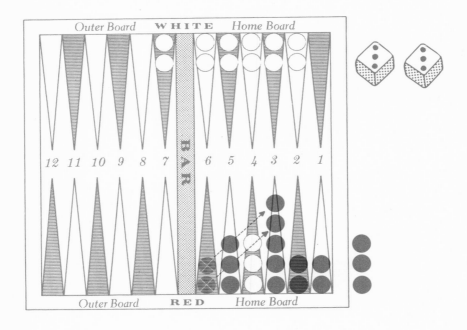

White owns your 4-point, which inhibits the movement of your men on the 6-point and 5-point. A total of five numbers; 6–2, 6–6, 5–5, and 4–4 leave a shot. You throw 3–3. What is the best way to play this throw? First, follow the rule of clearing your points in descending order by using two of the 3s to clear your 6-point as shown by the dotted line. Since the question is whether or not to move a man from your 5-point to begin clearing that point, let's use the third 3 to bear a man off the 3-point. If you use the last 3 to

104

bear off another man, leaving three men on your 5-point, six numbers (6–5, 6–4, and 5–4), leave a shot at your next turn. If you move a man from the 5-point to the 2-point, only four numbers (6–1 and 5–1) leave a shot. A further advantage: if your next throw does not include a 1 you can clear your 5-point immediately. Therefore, using the fourth 3 to move a man from the 5-point to the 2-point is obviously superior.

In general, when you are trying to clear a point, keep an even number of men on that point. If you are able to clear your points without leaving a blot, you may even gammon White in this position.

The contact game is usually a bad bet for the blocker with men on only one point, since even if he does get one shot — and there's no guarantee that he will — he will be bucking better than 2 to 1 odds against hitting the blot. In addition, he is running the very real risk of losing a double game (gammon) perhaps even a triple game (backgammon).

VI The doubling cube: key to winning

IF KNOWLEDGE of deployment is the heart of backgammon, the strategic management of the doubling cube is its soul. The cube, a comparatively recent innovation in so ancient a game, has added a new dimension of excitement and suspense that is primarily responsible for backgammon's burgeoning popularity. Here's how it works.

Each face of the doubling cube bears a number to record progressive doubles and redoubles: 2, 4, 8, 16, 32, and 64. Before play begins, the cube is placed between the players to the left or right of the board. Either player has access to the cube. Assume that you are playing for one unit. A unit might be any amount of money, oil wells, or match sticks. At his turn and before he throws the dice, either player may offer to double the stake by turning the cube to 2. His opponent may:

1] Decline the double, pay one unit, and start a new game or:
2] Accept, in which case the stake for the game becomes two units.

If the double is accepted, the doubled player "owns the cube." This means that only he has the option to redouble the game. He does so before any of his subsequent moves by turning the cube to 4. His opponent has the option of declining the redouble, paying two units (the last value of the cube) and starting a new game, or accepting, in which case the base stake becomes four units and the redoubled player gains ownership of the cube. In theory, this doubling and redoubling practice can go on forever. In practice, the cube is seldom doubled beyond 8 in games between experienced competitors.

Originally, the cube was introduced strictly as a gambling device. Today, the offer of a double and the decision of whether to accept or decline have been transformed into a science, which we will explore in this chapter.

It stands to reason that when a player offers a double he must

106

hold a positional advantage since future control of the cube is a tangible, and sometimes negotiable, asset. How much of an advantage should you have to double? How much of a disadvantage can you afford and still accept a double? Consider the interesting paradox illustrated by this diagram.

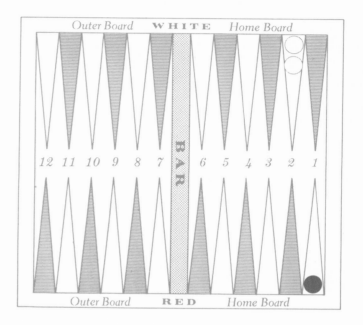

It is White's turn to throw. Twenty-six numbers bear off his last two men; only ten numbers fail to bear off. He turns the cube to 2. White's double is completely correct so, of course, you decline.

Right? *Wrong!*

When the doubling cube made its advent, one writer stated categorically that if a double was proper, it should be declined. This is complete nonsense. Much of the fascination of the cube rests in the paradox that a completely correct double can provide a completely proper acceptance.

Let's use a little simple arithmetic to prove that you should accept this double.

If you decline, you lose one unit. If you accept and White rolls one of his twenty-six good numbers, you lose two units. If White rolls one of his ten bad numbers, you will win two units. Since a pass automatically costs you one unit (-1) while an acceptance risks an additional unit to win two units $(+2)$, it can be seen that you are risking one unit for a potential gain of three additional units (the difference between —1 and +2). This means that, in effect, you are receiving 3 to 1 odds. Now let's analyze White's equity. Of the thirty-six possible throws, ten throws cost him the game. He is a 26 to 10 favorite or 2.6 to 1 to win the game. Since 2.6 to 1 is less than 3 to 1, you should accept the double.

CONCLUSION A: *You should accept any double when you are less than a 3 to 1 underdog.*

CONCLUSION B: *You should double when you are better than a 2 to 1 favorite.*

The difference between the 2 to 1 double and the 3 to 1 acceptance is proper.

Before considering the practical aspects of the cube in the three basic game types (the straight race, the back game, and the positional game), glance over the following probability tables. These are strictly for reference and need not be memorized. The few comments at the end of each table, however, will be helpful in general play.

TABLE I — *Odds of hitting a blot*

Distance in points	Odds against hitting	Hit %
1	25 to 11	31
2	24 to 12 or (2 to 1)	33
3	22 to 14 or (11 to 7)	39
4	21 to 15 or (7 to 5)	42
5	21 to 15 or (7 to 5)	42
6	19 to 17	47
7	30 to 6 or (5 to 1)	17
8	30 to 6 or (5 to 1)	17
9	31 to 5	14
10	33 to 3 or (11 to 1)	8
11	34 to 2 or (17 to 1)	6
12	33 to 3 or (11 to 1)	8
16	35 to 1	3
20	35 to 1	3
24	35 to 1	3

General conclusions if you must leave a blot.

A] *Any direct shot will be hit more often than any indirect shot.*

B] *For any direct shot — the closer you are, the less likely your blot will be hit.*

C] *For any indirect shot — the further away you are, the less*

108

likely your blot will be hit (the only exception is that a blot eleven points away is less likely to be hit than a blot twelve points away).

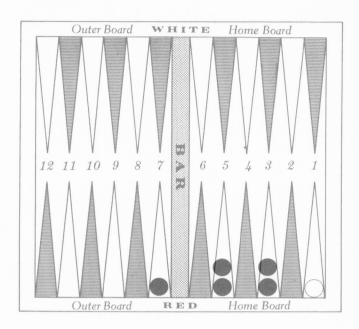

In each of these calculations, it is assumed that no throw is blocked. For instance, in the above position, two of the numbers that would hit your blot (4–2 and 2–4) are blocked. The odds must be adjusted from 19 to 17 to 21 to 15.

TABLE II — *Odds of re-entering a man from the bar*

Number of closed home board points	Expectation of re-entering	%
1	35 to 1	97
2	8 to 1	88
3	3 to 1	75
4	5 to 4	56
5	11 to 25	31

General conclusion from the table:

A] *In all cases, except when five home board points are closed, you are a favorite to re-enter a man from the bar.*

B] *Even when you have only one possible re-entry point, you can expect to re-enter approximately one out of three times.*

TABLE III — *Probability of bearing off your last two men in one throw*

Points on which men are located	# of throws	%
1 – 2	36	100
1 – 4	29	81
2 – 2	26	72
3 – 2	25	69
5 – 2	19	53
4 – 3	17	47
5 – 3	14	39
5 – 4	10	28
6 – 3	10	28
6 – 4	8	22
6 – 5	6	17
6 – 6	4	11

General conclusion from the table:
A] *The closer you are to the 1-point (the lower the pip count), the better your chances.*
B] *With equal pip count, your chances are usually better when one of the men is closer to the 1-point.*
e.g. compare 5–2 (53%) to 4–3 (47%) or
4–1 (81%) to 3–2 (69%)
Now that we've gotten past statistics, let's analyze the use of the doubling cube in each of the game types.

A. The straight race

IN THE SECTION on bearing off, you were introduced to the idea of counting the pips as an index to whether you are ahead or behind in the race. Pip counting is critical when dealing with the doubling cube because you are able to determine exactly *how you stand in any racing position.* It is important to realize that the measure of your lead is directly related to how many throws remain in the game. As an example, if both sides have removed most of their men from the board, the fact that it is your turn to throw may be sufficient justification to "turn the cube." On the other hand, a race where both sides are still struggling to bring men into their home board may not warrant a double, even if you are 10 or 15 pips ahead. Examine these two diagrams.

110

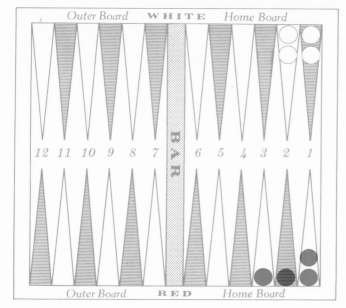

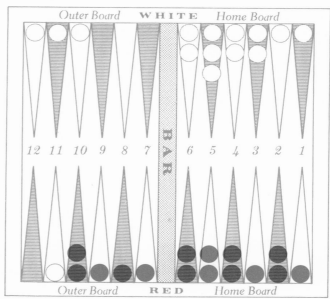

Diagram A shows a position where you (Red) are one pip behind yet you hold an overwhelming advantage if it is your turn. Unless you throw two 2-1s in a row, you will remove all of your men in
two turns. Barring doublets, White also needs two turns to remove
his men. Assuming it is your throw, you should double. As a general

111

rule when the combined pip count of both sides is less than 60, you should begin to calculate how many throws are left to the game. In the other diagram you are 9 pips ahead (91 to 82), yet a double at this point would be premature since there is still a long way to go.

Specifically, then, how far ahead should you be to double? Or, conversely, how far behind must you be to pass? The following table is designed to guide your judgment in close situations. The column at the left shows your present pip total. The column at the right gives the pip count difference at which a double is mandatory strategy and also, the outside limit at which the double should be accepted. The middle column indicates the pip advantage required to consider doubling.

TABLE IV — *Pip lead in the race*

Your pip total	Consider a double	Mandatory double
100 or more	15+	20+
80 – 100	12+	16+
70 – 79	9+	12+
60 – 69	6+	8+

In each of the above cases, the pip total coupled with the mandatory double column makes the game approximately a 3 to 1 proposition. Thus, if you have a pip count of 75, and your opponent has a pip count of 87, you are a 3 to 1 favorite. On the other hand, if his pip count is 63, you are a 3 to 1 underdog. Obviously, if his lead is less than 12 pips, you should usually accept the double. In situations where accepting or declining seem to be a tossup, your decision should be based on how well your position is diversified in relation to your opponent's. In each of the following diagrams, you are behind by 8 pips — 65 to 73. Your opponent doubles. In which position should you accept; in which position should you decline?

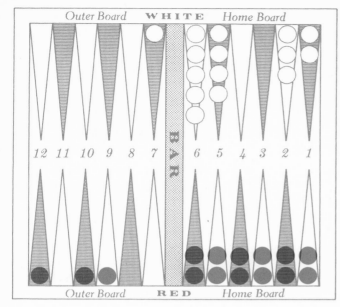

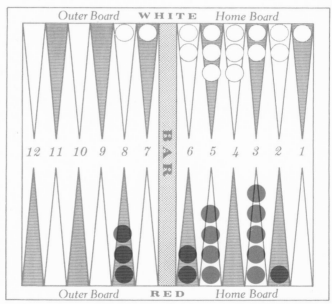

In the left hand diagram, Red should accept. In the other, Red should decline. The key lies in the diversification or "smoothness" of the home board positions. In the first example, you will miss few times since you are well diversified in your home board. After you bring home the three men in your outer board, you will have few problems bearing off; a 4 will remove a man from the 4-point, a 3 will remove a man from the 3-point and so on. White, on the other hand, is likely to have problems because as long as he has men on his 6-point and 5-point, every time he throws a 4 or a 3, he will not be able to remove a man. Notice that any 4 will be particularly harmful since he can neither remove a man nor fill the vacancies on his 4-point or 3-point.

In the other diagram, your open 4-point and 1-point make it very likely that you will waste throws. White, on the other hand, is nicely diversified.

Diversification is an indication of the *quality* of your pip lead or pip deficit. Thus, in the first diagram, White has a *bad* 8 pip lead, while in the other, he has a *good* 8 pip lead. The decision to double with the pip lead indicated in the center column of Table IV is based on a comparable diversification.

In each of the following diagrams, you enjoy a lead in the race. In which should you double? When you do double, in which will it be correct for your opponent to accept?

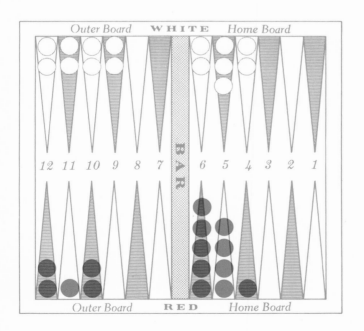

A

DIAGRAM A You have a healthy 10 pip lead, but your total of 109 pips (to 119 for White) means that there are too many throws remaining, and your double would be premature. When your count equals more that 100 pips, you should not consider doubling unless you are at least 15 pips ahead (TABLE IV). If you hold or increase your lead for the next two or three turns, doubling will become more attractive since your total pip count will be lower.

B

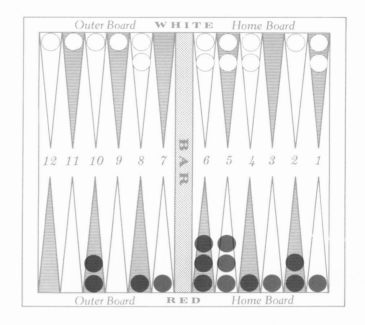

DIAGRAM B Your pip count is 79 while your opponent's pip count is 92. Your 13 pip lead means that a double may be considered but is not mandatory since your pip count is between 80 and 100 (TABLE IV). Since the double is far from the mandatory 16 pip lead, diversification should be considered. Although White has the disadvantage of an open 3-point, you are thin on your 4-point, 3-point, and 1-point. If you double, White will be sure to accept. We do not condemn an immediate double, but our preference is to wait one turn since we have little or no advantage in diversification. If you maintain the same approximate lead, double; it will be harder for White both to accept and to defeat you.

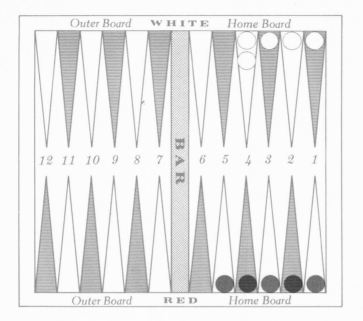

Outer Board   **WHITE**   Home Board

12 11 10 9 8 7   **BAR**   6 5 4 3 2 1

Outer Board   **RED**   Home Board

C

DIAGRAM C   Here, you are one pip behind but when the total pip count on the board falls below 60, specific throws should be considered. In this situation, the total pippage is 29 (15 for you; 14 for White). Each side should be able to remove its men in precisely three throws, and since it is your throw, you should double. Barring doublets or successive rolls of very low numbers such as 2–1 or 3–1, you will win the game. White should pass this double since he is approximately a 5 to 1 underdog.

116

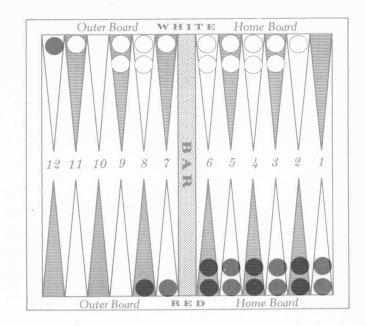

D

DIAGRAM D If your pip count is between 60 and 80, you should double automatically with a lead of 12 pips or more. In this case, your pip count is 70, and you are 20 pips ahead. Of course, you double and of course, White should pass.

SETTLEMENTS (optional)

While these next few pages are not absolutely necessary to skillful play, they will increase your knowledge of equities in relationship to backgammon itself.

As you will see later, any position where your opponent's runners have been permanently restrained has long since been doubled. Your opponent owns the cube and bases his winning hopes on your leaving a blot while bearing off. If you are hit and still have seven men to bear off, *he becomes a doubling favorite.* Many players do not like to risk victory or defeat on one lucky throw of the dice and will "settle the game" based on the equities involved. To clear up that last mouthful, assume that you threw a 5–4 to arrive at the position shown here.

117

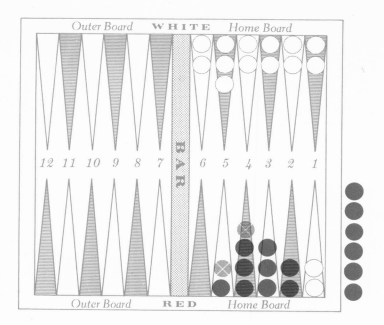

Your last 5–4 was most unfortunate since your only legal play, as marked by the ×s, left a direct shot. Assume that White owns the doubling cube at 2. If he throws a 4, thus hitting your blot, he will almost certainly redouble, in which case, you should decline and pay two units. If, on the other hand, he misses the blot, he will almost certainly lose and may, in fact, be gammoned. Neither side wants the result of the game to depend on one throw of the dice. Since eleven numbers hit while twenty-five numbers miss (see TABLE I), you are certainly a favorite and deserve some payment if this position is settled without a throw.

Calculating this is quite simple. The number of hits (win for White) cancel out some of the misses (lose for White). Therefore, subtract the number of hits from the number of misses. In this case, 25 misses — 11 hits = 14. Divide this number by the total number of possible throws (36). The result is approximately 39. Multiply this number by the size of the cube (in this case, 2), and the result will be your expectancy, or equity in this game. Assuming you are gambling for $1.00 a point, the final result of .78 means that with the cube at 2, (thus increasing the stakes of this particular game to $2.00), you are entitled to .78 cents as a fair settlement. If this position were repeated over a period of time, you would win an average of .78 cents per game.

A picture is worth a thousand words, and in this case, the picture is an algebraic one. Thus let M = a miss, H = a hit and C = the money represented by the cube. Now the settlement problem (excluding gammons) can be stated as $\dfrac{M - H}{36} \times C$

GAMMON POTENTIAL POSES DIFFERENT PROBLEMS.

The formula for calculating a win versus a gammon is:

$$\frac{M \times H/2}{36} \times 2C$$

Let's try "plugging" the right numbers into the gammon formula in the following diagram.

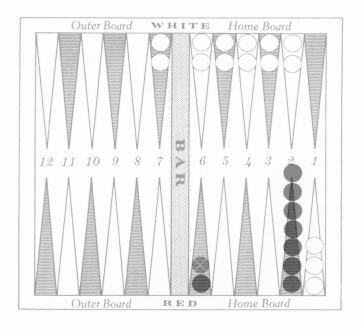

The cube is at 2, and the stakes are a hefty $10 a point. You just threw 5–1 and removed a man from the 6-point (as indicated by the ×.) If White misses, he is almost certain to be gammoned; if he hits, he is very likely to win. Assuming that he expresses a desire to settle the game, determine approximately what you are entitled to:

He has fifteen ways to hit you. Plugging the correct numbers into the formula we get:

$$\frac{20 - \dfrac{15}{2}}{36} \times \$40.00 \quad or \quad \frac{11.5}{36} \times \$40.00$$

Ît is customary to round off fractions in favor of the underdog, so we get:

$$\frac{12}{36} \times \$40.00 \quad or \quad \frac{1}{3} \times \$40.00.$$

The arithmetic boils down to 13.33 which means that you have an equity of $13.33 in this game. The game, in a practical situation, would be settled at either $13.00 or 13.50, depending on who was greedier or richer.

What should you (Red) pay as a maximum settlement in the following position? Remember, you must determine whether or not you are in danger of being gammoned to decide which formula to use. The stakes are $5.00 a point, and the cube is at 4.

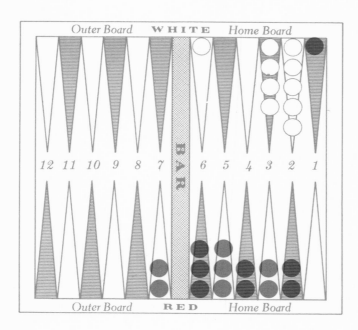

As you are in little danger of being gammoned, the simpler formula, $\dfrac{M - H}{36} \times C$ should be used. A total of 15 out of a possible

36 throws hit the White blot and the stake of the game is $20.00 ($5 × 4). The result is therefore, $\frac{21 - 15}{36} \times 20.00$ or $\frac{1}{6} \times 20.00$.

By dividing 6 into 20 dollars, you determine that White is entitled to $3.33 as his equity. If he asks you for more, throw the dice and try to win the game; he's either trying to take advantage of you, or he doesn't understand settlements.

If you had little or no trouble with this last problem, you should, with very little practice, become quite expert at the settlement process.

IN THE COMPLEX maneuvering and jockeying for position inherent in the back game and in the various forms of the positional game, a knowledge of your objectives goes hand in hand with a knowledge of when to use the cube. The one overriding principle is:

The non-racing game

Double the game whenever your opponent's situation includes an irreparable flaw.

Let's look at a series of five positions where it is correct strategy for you to double, based on this general principle.

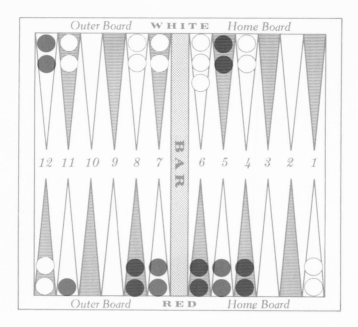

12 11 10 9 8 7   *6 5 4 3 2 1*

You have successfully advanced your own runners while setting up a near-prime to block White's runners. Since you have achieved both of your objectives while he has merely managed to set up a partial blockade of your runners in his outer board, there is a huge strategic flaw in his position. White should decline a double unless he is very rich, out of his mind, or has a secret pact with the goddess of luck and expects to throw 2–2 followed by 6–6 to liberate his runners.

122

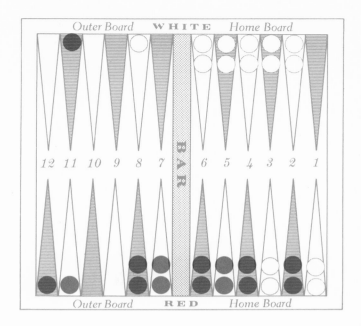

White has played a back game. A successful back game depends on both maintaining two points in your home board and an imposing position on his own home board. He has thus far maintained both of these requirements but an analysis of the position reveals an irreparable flaw in the White situation. This flaw is *timing*. You have three "spare men" on your 11-point, 12-point, and the White 10-point. This means that you can move around the board for three or four throws without disturbing your blockading structure. What about White? He has one spare man (on his bar-point), after which he will have the dubious choice of releasing one of his points in your home board (with a 6) or breaking up his own home board. He is badly mistimed and the double is a standout.

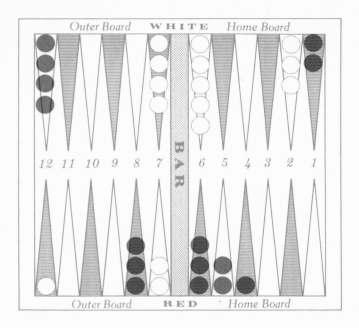

In this grotesque position, White threw a 6–6 twice in succession — certainly an asset in a straight race, but this is hardly a racing position. He has many serious weaknesses. The three men on his 2-point, your shot at his man on your 12-point and most important, his inability to escape scot free from your bar-point without throwing yet another doublet. You, on the other hand, are about to make your 4-point and have a great deal of freedom of movement. From a practical point of view, he will have to leave a shot on almost every throw. Red's double, while aggressive, is certainly correct. White will have to do a great deal of very clever (and lucky) squirming to win the game.

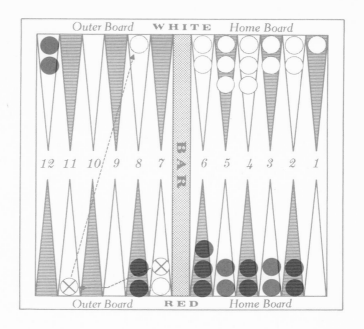

Outer Board **WHITE** Home Board

12 11 10 9 8 7 **BAR** 6 5 4 3 2 1

Outer Board **RED** Home Board

In this position, where you had been holding White's two men prisoner on your bar-point, his throw of 6–4 has forced him to move a man from your bar-point (his only legal play). Since twenty-four throws hit the "lonesome stranger" on your bar-point, while only twelve throws miss, you start out as an immediate 2 to 1 favorite to win. (Obviously, if you hit the blot, your powerful home board leaves White very little hope). Even if you fail to hit, most of the 11 pips you are behind in a straight race should be made up by your next throw. Therefore, you still have a solid equity in the race. White should accept this double, since he is not a 3 to 1 underdog. This delicate position sets the stage for an old refrain of the doubling cube: "If I must lose to an unlucky series of throws, you must pay for the privilege of forcing me to roll."

Paradoxically, there are times when it is incorrect to double because your position is too strong. As an example, consider this diagram:

125

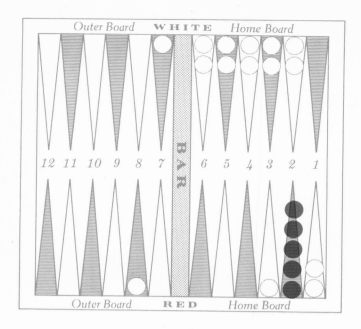

In this position, resulting from a White back game, you have been able to remove the Red men without incident from all points except the 2-point. Even if you leave a shot and this shot is hit, you will still be a favorite to win the game. For all of that, if you happen to own the cube, it would be an error to double since White would gratefully decline, avoiding the almost certain gammon. Assume that you remove four of your men and your last man is hit. You can then use the doubling cube since with so many men off, you should be able to re-enter your man from the bar while White is bearing off, and win the race easily.

The principle is, *when you have complete control, don't double as long as you have chances to gammon your opponent.* As an example from the middle game, consider the following position in the flash light of the doubling cube.

126

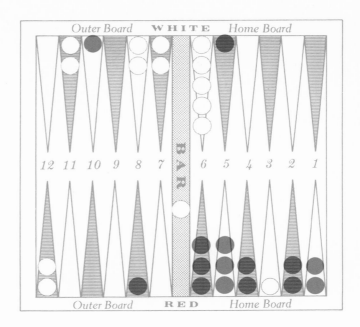

Red has a tremendous advantage, yet to double would be throwing away money as White would certainly pass. With five points closed on your home board and a White piece on the bar, you should bend every effort to make your 3-point before he can re-enter. If you are able to successfully shut White out, closing your board and placing two of his men on the bar, a little care should make the gammon an almost sure thing. Proper strategy would be to hit White's man on your 3-point (leaving a blot if necessary) and attempt to close the point. Later, if White is able to make your 3-point, his position will probably remain sufficiently untenable for you to double confidently.

At this point, we will end our discussion of the doubling cube. In the next chapter, we will present actual games played between expert contestants and will observe the cube used in relation to the position as it develops.

Illustrative games

We have presented the elements and rules of backgammon, the opening moves, the principles of strategy, of
bearing off, and finally of the doubling cube. In these chap-
ters, we are going to tie this package together by presenting
games between acknowledged experts. Here, you will see the
development and deployment of the opposing armies as controlled by the dice. When either side falls on hard times, the
doubling cube will be brought into play.

To make these games easy to follow, each move is diagrammed. In each case, the diagram represents the position
after the indicated throw has been moved.

As usual, you are conducting the Red forces against the
White "bad guys."

VII The straight race

AS YOU KNOW, the object of the straight race is to bring your men home as quickly as possible, utilizing the principles of economy and diversification as a guide for your movements. When involved in a straight race, the successful backgammon player is aware at all times of how he stands in the race; he counts the pips with an eye to doubling or being doubled.

In this game, special attention should be paid to the use of the doubling cube. You (Red) will be required to exercise judgment both in relation to your moves, and to the use of the cube. Refer to the table in Chapter VI (the cube), which tells when to double in a race. Try to determine the proper move for each of your throws before reading the text. As you enter the stretch run, analyze your position and work out whether you are ahead or behind by counting the pips.

w1. 6 – 4
Move a runner to
the Red 11-point.

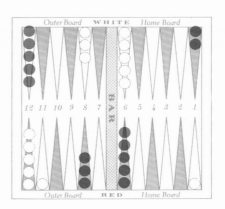

White plays his opening throw in the recommended manner by trying to escape with one of his runners.

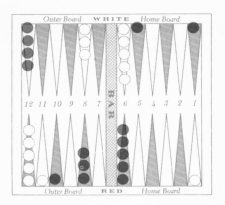

Move a runner to the White 5-point. Move a man to your 10-point.

Since you were unable to throw a 2, hitting the runner on your 11-point, you make the recommended opening move which simultaneously brings a builder to your outer board and threatens to take over the White 5-point.

w2. 6 – 4

Move a runner to the Red 11-point.

By making Red's 11-point, White has created a safe haven for both of his runners and thus, has achieved at least a temporary opening advantage.

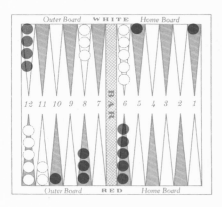

R2. 5 – 5

Move your runner on the White 5-point to your own 5-point. Move the man on your 10-point to your 5-point.

An unusual way to make the 5-point! With this play, you have safetied one of your runners and made a key point. Making the 5-point is clearly superior to the customary treatment of 5–5, which makes the rather unimportant 3-point.

132

w3. 6 – 1

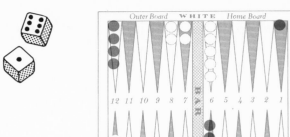

Move a man from the Red 12-point to the White bar-point.

Move a man from the White 8-point to the White bar-point.

A very good throw. Red's runner on the White 1-point is now in real danger of being blockaded. Since there are no White runners left to restrain, Red's first order of business will be to try to move his lonesome runner to safety.

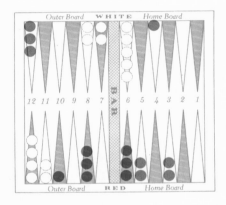

R3. 3 – 3

Move your runner to the White 4-point.

Move two men from your 6-point to your 3-point.

Move a man from the White 12-point to your 10-point.

This unusual treatment of a doublet is based on sound strategy. As we indicated in our discussion of White's third turn, your runner should be brought to safety as quickly as possible. By moving your runner to the 4-point, you threaten to jump over the White blockade with either a 5 or a 6. Making the 3-point has the subtle purpose of deterring White from leaving a blot while hitting your runner, since you've constructed the beginnings of an ominous home board. The fourth 3 is used to bring a builder for the 4-point to your outer board.

133

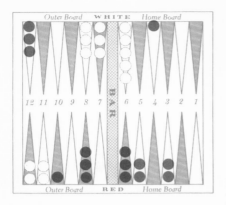

w4. 6 – 5

Move a man from the Red 12-point to the White bar-point.

Move a man from the Red 12-point to the White 8-point.

Since White cannot attack Red's runner, he brings two men safely to his outer board, thus providing builders against Red's runner should he fail to escape. White now threatens to make inner points without leaving blots on his bar-point or 8-point. Red needs a good number.

r4. 6 – 2

Move your runner to the White 10-point.

Continue with the same man to the White 12-point.

A clutch throw at the right time! By safetying your runner, you have obviated the many White blockading threats against the runner. Notice that the usually desirable play of making your 4-point by moving men from your 10-point and your 6-point would not meet the most pressing need of the position since your runner would still be in danger.

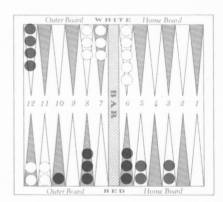

Both sides have freed their runners without incident. Although there is still a bit of mutual restraint between your men on the White 12-point and White's on the Red 11-point and 12-point, it should be no problem for either side to by-pass these tiny obstacles. For this reason, the game is now practically a non-contact race. When you have determined that a game has devolved into a race, the first thing is to count the pips to find out whether you are ahead or behind.

A pip count tells us that Red is 9 pips ahead (120 to 129). But it is White's turn to throw, so the race is virtually even and there is no question of either side doubling this game just yet.

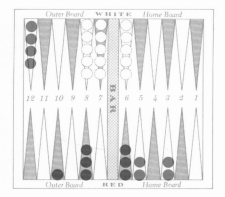

w5. 6 – 6
Move two men from the Red 11-point to the White 8-point.
Move two men from the Red 12-point to the White bar-point.

Ouch! White gains 24 pips by throwing the best number that can be rolled in a race. With this bombshell, the lead changes hands.

135

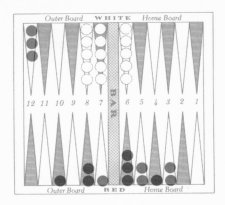

R5. 6 – 4

Move a man from the White 12-point to your bar-point.

Move a man from your 8-point to your 4-point.

This over-average racing number is good enough to keep you very much alive. Note the technique of bringing your men home. You bring a man to your bar-point with the 6 to diversify your outer board so that your men can be brought in with maximum economy. The 4 is used to place a man on your vacant 4-point in preparation for bearing off. Non-doublets ideally remove two men a turn; one for each die. Vacant points can lead to wasted throws — e.g., if the 4-point is open, and you throw a 4, you will have to move a man from your 5-point or 6-point.

WHITE DOUBLES

It is hard to conceal your surprise at White's double. Perhaps he felt that his previous 6–6 was of sufficient psychological value to induce you to pass. It is time to count the pips again, just to make sure.

White's pip count is 105, while yours is 110. In the chapter on the cube, we learned that a 20 pip lead is usually required for a sound double when both sides have more than 100 pips to go. White's 5 pip lead certainly does not make him a 3 to 1 favorite. In fact, considering your relative diversifications, it is doubtful whether he is a favorite at all. Of course, you accept the double. There are a lot of throws left.

w6. 3 – 3

Move 2 men from the White 8-point to the White 5-point.

Move 2 men from the White bar-point to the White 4-point.

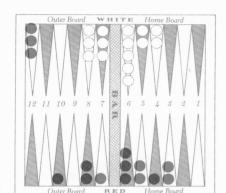

With this good throw, White is able to move 4 men into his home board. He does so in proper fashion by diversifying on his 5-point and 4-point. He has increased his lead to 17 pips.

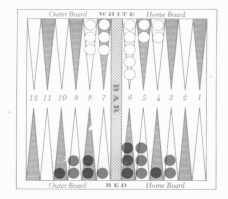

R6. 4 – 4

Move 3 men from the White 12-point to your 9-point.

Move 1 man from your 9-point to your 5-point.

With this timely throw, you pick up 16 pips and move within 1 pip of your opponent. After you brought the 3 men to your outer board from the White 12-point, you had to choose between moving a man from your 8-point to your 4-point or making the indicated move. While it would be pleasant to put an extra man on your 4-point, thus further smoothing out your home board, the diversification in your outer board would suffer. The awkward pileup of 3 men on your 9-point could result in a waste of a turn bringing the remaining men home.

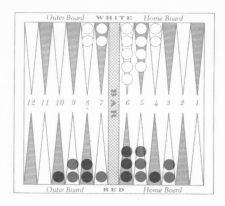

w7. 3 – 2

Move a man from the White 8-point to the White 5-point.

Move a man from the White bar-point to the White 5-point.

White does the best he can with this under-average racing number by moving 2 men from his outer board to the 5-point. You may be sure that White is sorry he gave up the cube in such an over-hasty fashion just two moves ago.

R7. **6 – 5**

Move a man from your 8-point to your 2-point.

Move a man from your 9-point to your 4-point.

This racing number is the best of the non-doublets. Pay special attention to how your home board position has improved while you've maintained healthy diversification in your outer board.

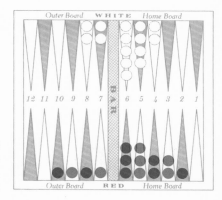

138

w8. 2 – 1

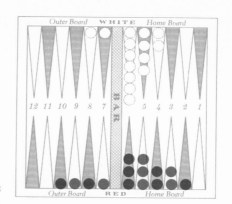

Move a man from the White 8-point to the White 6-point.

Move a man from the White bar-point to the White 6-point.

White continues to roll badly. He does what he can with meager racing resources by bringing two men into his home board. One of the problems in throwing low dice in a race is that it is difficult to diversify while bringing men home.

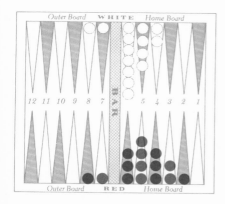

r8. 6 – 4

Move a man from your 10-point to your 4-point.

Move a man from your 9-point to your 5-point.

It is undesirable to further diversify your home board by bringing men to your 2-point and 1-point at the expense of leaving a "gap" in your outer board. Therefore, you employ the principal of economy by bringing home those men furthest from your home board.

POSITION AFTER RED'S 6-4

Before the throw, you were 2 pips ahead with the smoother position. Now you are 12 pips ahead (73 to 85) and, if your lead holds up, you will be in the range to redouble. Remember that, as the pip count decreases, you need a shorter lead to double. Assuming normal throws, time is on your side.

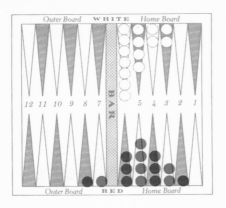

w9. 5 – 4

Move a man from the White 8-point to the White 3-point.

Move a man from the White bar-point to the White 3-point.

White is able to move his last 2 men home in diversified fashion for the first time in three moves. He is struggling in an inferior position and to add to his troubles, you own the cube and he therefore has a potential redouble hanging over his head. White is now 3 pips behind.

r9. 3 – 3

Move a man from your 8-point to your 5-point.

Move a man from your bar-point to your 4-point.

Remove the 2 men from your 3-point.

With this doublet, you have not only achieved a 15 pip lead, you have gained a head start in the bearing off process.

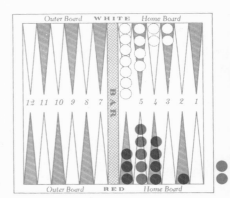

140

w10. 4 – 3

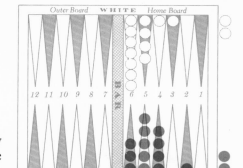

Remove a man from the White 4-point.

Remove a man from the White 3-point.

White begins the bearing off process by removing the two men indicated by the dice.

POSITION AFTER WHITE'S 4–3

It's time for you to count the pips again. You are ahead by 8 pips (61 to 69). Technically, you should redouble but in this case, the Red player decided that since his opponent was so aggressive, as evidenced by his original double, he could afford to "wait a turn" before redoubling. He was afraid that White would accept the redouble but his reasoning was falacious since he should *want* White to accept the redouble. After all, it's better to win four units than it is to win two units. Of course, if you were playing this game, you would redouble immediately since you've become familiar with the equities of the doubling cube and are armed with the table on page 112.

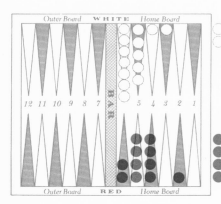

r10. 6 – 5

Remove a man from your 6-point.

Remove a man from your 5-point.

You make the forced move which, incidentally, is a good racing number.

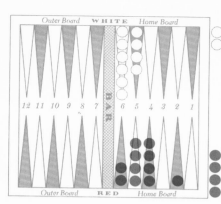

w11. 6 – 3
*Remove a man
from the White 6-
point.
Remove a man
from the White 3-
point.*

White makes his forced move by re-moving two men.

RED REDOUBLES

The new pip count is 50 to 60. You are 10 pips ahead with not many throws left to the game. White is more than a 3 to 1 underdog and must pass. Surprisingly enough, White counted the pips and seemed torn about whether to accept or decline his awful racing position. After a long huddle, White announced that he would take the "conservative view" and declined the redouble! You have won two units, yet if you had redoubled on your ninth turn it is likely, judging from the temperament of your opponent, that he would have accepted the redouble and most probably lost four units. Timid use of the cube is as expensive as over-zealous doubling. This is usually not obvious since the conservative doubler is likely to win the game anyway. Consider the diagram of the following hypothetical race.

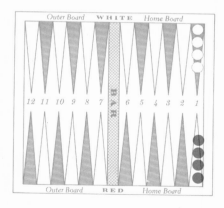

Assuming it is your throw, it is evident that you have a great advantage. Whether or not you double, you are better than a 5 to 1 favorite to win since even if you fail to throw a doublet, there are only six numbers (the doublets) out of thirty-six that will pull the game out for White. By doubling, you force White to play for twice the stakes if he wants to try to win. It stands to reason that he will decline the double rather than play for such a small equity. If you fail to double, you are giving your opponent a "free" 16% chance to beat you. It doesn't happen very often, but it can happen! If he accepts the cube and should happen to win, smile. Enough acceptances like this will make you a big winner in the long run.

CONCLUSION — *Backgammon is very much a game of percentages. Make those percentages work in your favor.*

VIII The positional game

THE positional game, best described as the *mutual holding game*, can take many forms. In general, its characteristics are:

1] Each side has an advanced point (or points) in the opponent's home board.

2] Each side has an effective blockade against his opponent's advanced points.

The prime objective is to try to escape unscathed with your runners. The most effective way to escape would be by throwing an appropriate doublet. Another way to escape would be to hit an opponent's blot, since he must use half of his next move to re-enter. It is very dangerous to try to escape with a single runner since the remaining runner will be vulnerable to attack. (Remember, the blockading points in your opponent's outer board also serve as builders for his home board).

To make running more dangerous for the enemy, each side attempts to make points in his home board while maintaining his blockade.

Let's play a typical positional game. To test your skill, decide how you would play each throw for both sides before reading the actual moves we will make.

r1. 4 – 3

*Move a runner to
the White 5-point.
Move a man to
your 10-point.*

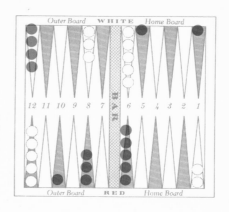

This is the recommended opening play. With this throw you simultaneously challenge the White 5-point and move a builder to your outer board.

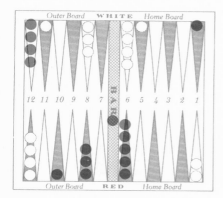

w1. 2 – 1

*Move a man to the
White 11-point.
Hit Red's blot on
the 5-point.*

White hits your blot on his 5-point to prevent your covering with a 4 on the next throw. The 2 brings a man to White's outer board for building purposes.

r2. 5 – 3

*You re-enter with
the 5, hitting
White's blot.
Cover your builder
on the 10-point.*

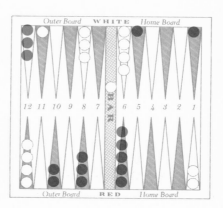

This throw would have been better if you did not have a man on the bar, as you would have been able to make your 5-point. However, you did well to hit the White man, forcing him to start over in your home board.

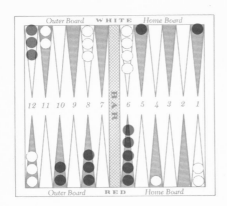

w2. 4 — 2

White re-enters on Red's 4-point.

Cover the builder on White's 11-point.

White could not hit your runner on his 5-point, so he did the next best thing by covering the builder in his outer board.

r3. 4 — 3

Move your runner to the White 5-point.

Move a man to your 10-point.

You have achieved the objective of your first move: you now own White's 5-point. The 3 is used to bring another builder to your 10-point.

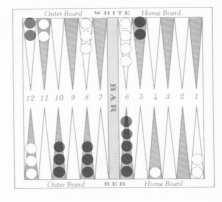

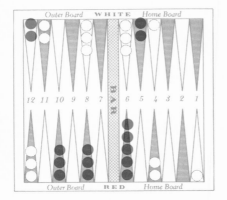

w3. 3 — 2

Move a runner to Red's 4-point.

Move a man to White's 4-point.

A mutual holding position has been established. Both sides have created advanced outposts in their opponent's home board. Your outpost on the 5-point is blockaded by his 11-, 8- and 6-points. White's outpost on your 4-point is blockaded by your 10-, 8- and 6-points. Notice that the advanced outposts reduce the blocking value of the key points (bar-point and 5-point). The blockade points are now those located in the outer board. Nevertheless, your immediate aims are to make your bar-point and your 5-point. White's primary target is his bar-point — but not at the expense of giving up his 11-point which serves to hold your runners if, for example, you were to throw 6–6. In this early stage of the game, you have a slight advantage because your point is more advanced than White's point. However, this advantage is minuscule and winning or losing will depend primarily on good technique.

The future strategy of both sides involves constructing points in the home board to inhibit the movement of the enemy runners. The threat is that if either player tries to escape with one runner, his remaining runner will become a vulnerable blot to be hit or even to be pointed upon.

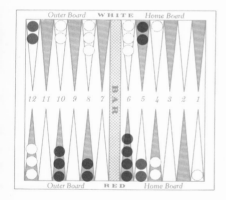

R4. 3 − 1
Move a man from your 8-point and a man from your 6-point, making the 5-point.

You have a choice of whether to make your 5-point or your bar-point. The 5-point is superior for two important reasons.

a] It makes a point in your home board.
b] It helps to diversify the "stacked up" men on your 6-point.

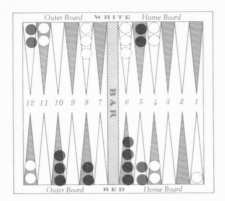

w4. 5 – 4
Move a man from the Red 12-point to the White 4-point.

This completes the aim of White's previous move, making his 4-point. As mentioned earlier, constructing useful points in the home board is important in a mutual holding game, inhibiting an attempted escape by a single runner.

R5. 3 – 2
Move a man to your 3-point.
Move a man to your 8-point.

Moving the 3 to your 3-point leaves a blot; nevertheless, it is the correct play. Since you are entrenched on White's 5-point, you should have no great problem re-entering if you are hit. Your prime objective at this point is to make your points in order and the 3-point is next. The play of the 2 creates an extra builder to cover your 3-point.

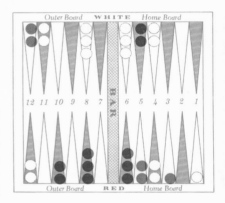

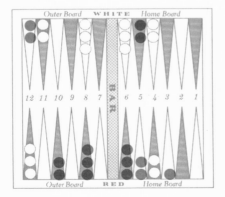

w5. 6 – 5
Move the single White runner to the safety of the 12-point.

White's "Lover's Leap" to safety brings an extra man into play against Red's runners.

148

R6. 6 – 3

*Move a man to
your 2-point.
Cover your man
on the 3-point.*

You continue correctly by making your 3-point and preparing to make your 2-point.

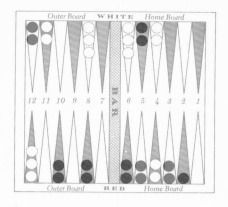

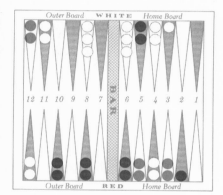

w6. 6 – 4

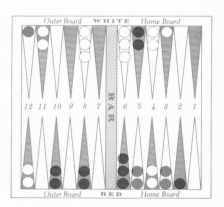

*Move a man from
Red's 12-point to
the White 3-point.*

White continues with a similar strategy aimed at making points in his home board to inhibit your runners.

R7. 4 – 3

*Move a man from
the White 12-
point to your 6-
point.*

A reply of 5–1 or 3–1 by White could be disastrous, but you should risk being hit in order to further your main objective: that is, containing the White runners.

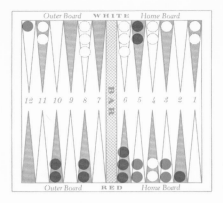

Move two men from Red's 12-point to the White 1-point.

Doublets are usually desirable throws but in a blockading game they can be disadvantageous when they cannot be used to escape with the runners. Because of this throw, White is going to have difficulty maintaining his blockade. The essence of a mutual holding game is timing, and White is now mistimed.

R8. 3 – 1

Move your man from the 6-point to the 2-point.

You continue your contiguous-point-making strategy by covering the 2-point.

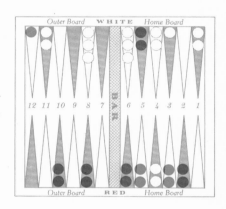

w8. 6 – 1

Move the men on the White 8- and 3-points to the White 2-point.

White makes a point in his inner board. Notice that he is running out of spare men to move and may soon be forced either to break up his blockade or to run with a man from your 4-point.

R9. 5 − 2

Move your man from the White 12-point to your 6-point.

Your spare man serves you well, allowing you to maintain both your blockade and your outpost in White's board.

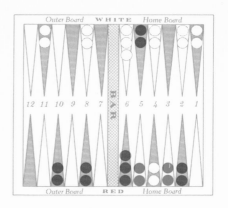

This situation illustrates advantageous *timing*. Your position is favorable because your outpost is more advanced. Your advantage is greater still because White has few "spare moves." It is likely that he will have either to break his outer board blockade or to abandon his outpost on his coming throw.

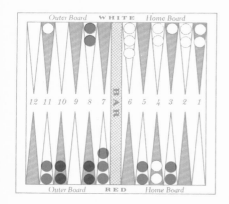

w9. 6 − 3

Move a man from the White 11-point to the 2-point.

Not the lucky throw White needed. He is faced with the disagreeable choice of breaking his blockade, simultaneously leaving a direct shot, or of running around the corner with one of his outpost men. He selected the superior alternative. (Running would leave the remaining White man on your 4-point too vulnerable to attack.) Having had to break his blockade put him at a severe disadvantage.

151

The cardinal rule for doubling in a positional game is that there must be a definite and preferably irreparable defect in your opponent's deployment. Not only was White forced to give up his blockade; you have many additional advantages to justify your double.

1] Of thirty-six possible throws, sixteen hit the blot on White's 11-point. If you hit this blot, you will be able to vacate your outpost with comparative safety (White must waste half of his move re-entering your formidable board). At the same time, you have taken a commanding lead in the race.

2] Your outpost is more advanced — 5-point vs. 4-point. Now that White has been forced to break his outer board blockade, the power of the advanced outpost will make itself felt. Examine the hypothetical future positions.

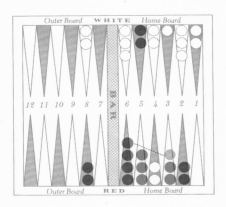

Hypothetical Position "A"

You've had very bad luck. Not only did you miss the shot, you were forced to break your 10-point while White was able to keep the blockade on his 8-point. You still have an appreciable advantage since you will be able to move both outpost men past the White position with ten throws (6–6, 5–5, 4–4, 2–2, 6–5, 6–4, and 5–4), while White has only five throws (6–6, 5–5, 3–3, and 6–5) that will let him escape.

3] Your timing is vastly superior. If you miss the direct shot, it is more likely that while you are forced to break your 10-point, White will be forced to break his 8-point, thus allowing both your men to escape with twenty-five numbers (anytime you do not throw a 1). White will then be reduced to an indirect shot to win the game. Consider hypothetical position B, a likely result, if you miss the original shot.

Hypothetical Position "B"

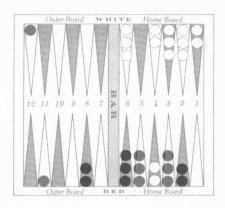

Since running with one outpost man is too dangerous, White must hit to win. In this situation, eleven numbers hit one of your blots; 6–1, 5–2, 4–3, 6–3, 5–4, and 3–3. This makes you a 25 to 11 bet not to be hit, meaning that you are better than 2 to 1 to win the game. Indeed, we are giving White his best potential: he has been able to hold a 5-point home board, while you might have been able to move your outpost men in a way that left fewer shots.

With so many disadvantages, White wisely declines the double, gives up the game and pays one unit.

IX The wipeout

IN GAME TYPES, we included the straight race, the positional or holding game, and the back game. The wipeout may be loosely classified as a positional game although, in reality, it belongs in a class by itself. The distinguishing feature of the wipeout is that one side tries to deliver an early knockout punch by simultaneously hitting blots and making home board points. The wipeout succeeds when the player who is hit has re-entry problems.

In the following game, Red conducts a classic wipeout attack. Just when it seems to be all over, White throws a sensational number which puts the game "up for grabs." Pay special attention to the handling of the doubling cube in this exciting game.

As usual, you are conducting the Red forces.

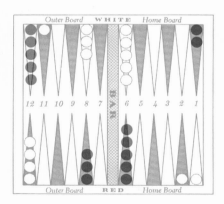

w1. 2 – 1
Move a man to the White 11-point. Move a runner to the 2-point.

White won the opening throw and plays it in recommended fashion, bringing a builder to his outer board and diversifying his runners.

154

R2. 5 – 5

Move two men to your 3-point.
Move two men to your 1-point, hitting the White blot.

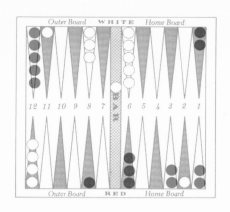

5–5 is the least desirable of doublets. An early 5–5 always involves making the 3-point. If the White runners were not split, you (Red) would have moved two of your men from the White 12-point to your 3-point. With the White runners activated, your correct strategy is to make two new points in your home board, simultaneously putting a White runner on the bar.

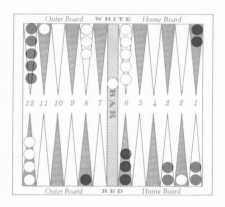

w2. 6 – 3

White fails to re-enter.

RED DOUBLES

This surprising double on the second move of the game is a speculative maneuver based on your intention to play for a wipeout. You hope to keep White off balance by hitting another blot and continuing to make points in your home board. Although you are by no means a solid favorite, you have a sound double. If your strategy succeeds, White is in serious danger of being gammoned.

However, if White is able to re-enter and establish either your 4-point or your 5-point, he will probably have the superior position. To understand why, consider the following hypothetical position which could arise in this game.

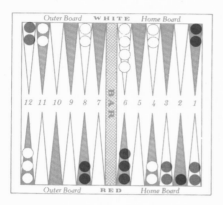

White controls your 4-point. The four men you used to make the 3-point and the 1-point are no longer available to make blocking points in your outer board. White will play to make up his home board and you will be hard pressed to bring your men around the track without leaving several shots. Since you are aware of this possibility, you will go all out to keep both White runners on the bar, thus gaining time to bring all of your men home. If your strategy succeeds, a wipeout is likely to result. Were it not for the gammon possibility hanging over White's head, the chances would be about equal for both sides. But if you succeed in gammoning White, you will win four units and this possibility swing the odds to favor your double. You must be prepared for the possibility that you may have to refuse a later redouble, but in doubling early, you risk one additional unit with a good chance to gain three.

R3. 6 – 5

Hit the White blot on your 2-point from the White 12-point.

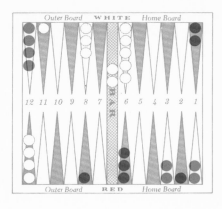

We are accustomed to using this "automatic" opening throw as a Lover's Leap to bring one runner to safety. However, you've decided to play for a wipeout, so you use any number to keep two White runners on the bar.

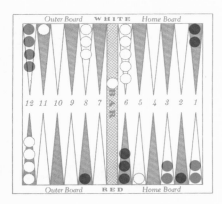

w3. 6 – 5

Re-enter one of the White men.

White is able to re-enter only one of his men from the bar.

R4. 4 – 3

Cover your 2-point with a man from your 6-point. Hit White's blot on your 5-point.

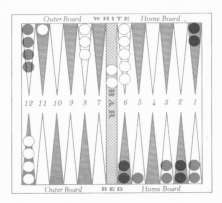

Continue your attacking plan. Close a fourth point on your home board and hit the White blot on your 5-point. (Note that you are disregarding the usual aim of making points that are not too far advanced in your home board). You are throwing good numbers but remember, you need good technique to take advantage of them.

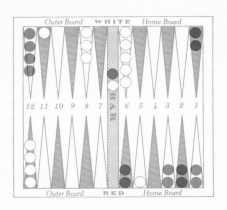

w4. 5 – 2

*White re-enters
one man, hitting
Red's blot.*

A good throw. White could come in
with only one of his men but in doing
so, he hit Red's 5-point blot. Red has
no men available in his outer board directly bearing on his 5-point. White
should have a good chance to re-enter his
second man from the bar because Red
must waste half his next throw in re-
entering.

r5. 4 – 4

*Re-enter your man.
Hit White's blot
on your 5-point.
'Move a builder to
your 9-point.*

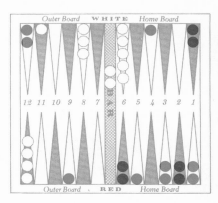

With this perfect throw, you do a lot
of good things at the same time. You
come off the bar, you hit White's blot
in your home board, and you move a
builder into position in your outer board.
Before this roll, White seemed to have
excellent recovery chances. After this
throw he is again in grave danger. One of
the thrills of backgammon is the speed
with which the fortunes of war can
change.

158

w5. 4 – 1

White re-enters one man.

Again, White can only bring in one of his men, and he does so on the poorer open point! He might have had good, though tenuous chances, had he again been able to hit the blot on your 5-point. As it stands, White is fast falling into deep trouble.

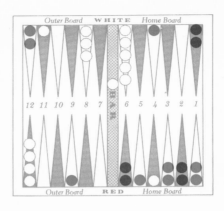

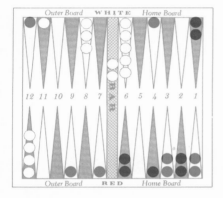

R6. 6 – 1

Bring a man to your bar-point. Use the ace to hit the blot on your 4-point.

You continue your wipeout plan, hitting the blot in your home board and scattering builders in your outer board, trying to make your 5-point and your 4-point.

w6. 6 – 6

Fails to re-enter.

This is a disastrous moment for White to stay on the bar. Since you are very likely to make your 4-point on your next throw, his situation is next to hopeless.

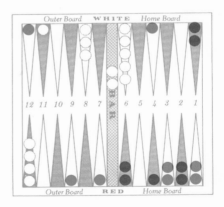

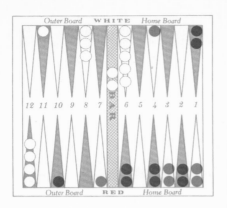

Cover your 4-point with your man from the 9-point. Move a builder to your 10-point.

You take the opportunity to make the fifth point on your home board and methodically bring another builder to your outer board. You are going all-out to make the 5-point, thus completing a prime in your home board.

w7. 4 − 4

Fails to re-enter.

One throw too late! On his previous turn, before you made the 4-point, this would have saved White.

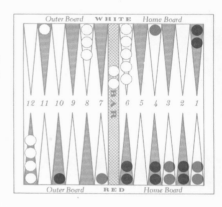

Move a runner to the White 11-point, hitting the blot.

To add injury to insult, you hit another White blot, putting a third man on the bar. However, a better choice would have been to provide another builder for the 5-point by moving your man on the White 4-point around the board to your 11-point.

160

Notice that every man White moved from its original position now rests on the bar. This position, which looks like one side has hardly moved, is typical of a successful wipeout strategy. You plan to continue diversifying men in your outer board, increasing the number of throws that will let you make your 5-point and close your home board. If you succeed, White will remain totally immobilized until you open points in your home board as you bear off. As he has men on the bar, you will be as careful as possible to avoid leaving a blot while you are bearing off. Then you will most certainly gammon him, for White will not be able to get a man off before you bear off all of yours.

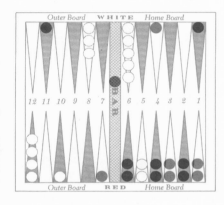

w8. 5 − 5

Re-enter the three White men on the bar.

Hit Red's blot on the 10-point.

With one foot in the grave, White produces a miraculous 35-to-1 shot to put him right back into the game. From a virtually certain gammon, White is suddenly in a situation where Red will need luck to bring his remaining men home.

r9. 6 − 3

Re-enter your man on the White 3-point.

Move a man to your 8-point.

You run around the corner with your man on the White outer board so that in order to hit, White will have to open your 5-point.

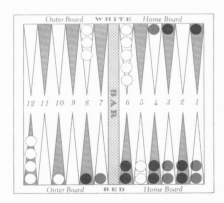

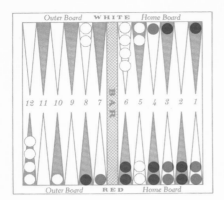

w9. 3 – 1

*Move two men
from the White 8-
and 6-points to the
White 5-point.*

This is much superior to hitting the man on Red's 8-point. To win the game, White must set up a blockade in his home board and making the 5-point helps to accomplish this.

r10. 5 – 1

*Run out to the
White 9-point.
Cover your blot on
the bar-point.*

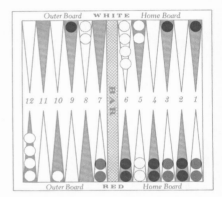

After safetying the men in your outer board, you begin the slow process of trying to extricate your three men from White's side of the board. Because you have no points in either outer board, your route home will be fraught with danger. It is vital to keep your home board intact so that White cannot expose blots without concern about reentering.

WHITE REDOUBLES

White's action is highly premature but psychologically understandable. Just two moves ago, White could look forward to being gammoned. Now he has an advantage in that he can, with moderately good throws, blockade your runners. None the less, White should wait until he has constructed at least one more blocking point before turning the cube to 4.

You are not happy at the turn of affairs but you accept the double. There is still a great deal of fight left in the position, and at least you now control the cube.

162

w10. 3 – 1

Move a man to the White 9-point, hitting Red's blot.

Not exactly the throw White hopes for. He hits the blot, hoping to cover on the next throw and increase his blockade. There are ten numbers you can throw that will hit this blot; 6–1, 6–2, 6–3, 6–4, and 5–4. Possibilities like this are part of the reason that his redouble was premature.

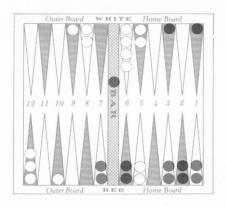

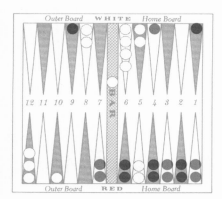

R11. 6 – 4

Re-enter with the 4.
Hit White's blot on the 9-point.

You have thrown one of the numbers that counterhit! The fortunes of war have shifted again. White is in trouble.

w11. 3 – 2

Fails to re-enter.

White is back in the situation he was in for most of the game, struggling to come in with a man on the bar and only one point open.

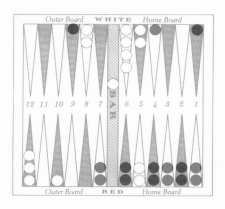

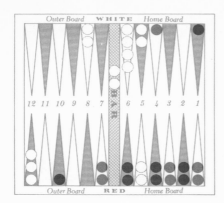

R*12.* 4 – 2

Hit the White blot on your 10-point.

You put another man upon the bar. At this point, your game is too good for you to turn the cube to 8. Once again you have good chances to gammon White and if you redouble, he will certainly pass to avoid that possibility.

w*12.* **6 – 1**

Fails to re-enter.

Every time White stays out, he comes closer to a gammon.

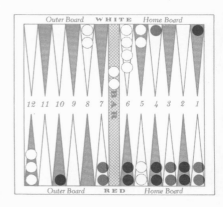

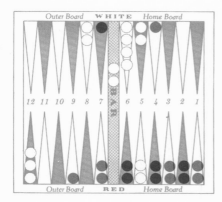

R*13.* 6 – 1

Move a man to the White bar-point. Move a man to your 9-point.

You begin the process of trying to bring your remaining men home by moving out to the White bar-point. With the memory of the last 5–5 thrown by White, you use the 1 to move your man "out of the way" in case he should throw another miracle number.

w13. 5 – 4

*White re-enters
one of his men.*

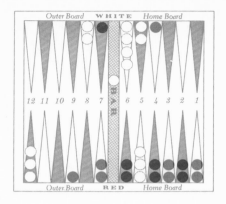

RED TURNS THE CUBE TO 8

Now that White has brought one man off the bar, you are apprehensive lest he re-enter his other man too quickly and jeopardize your race to your home board. It would be poor strategy to risk a sure four units for the possibility of winning eight units. Notice how the equities of the cube work in your favor — White must pass and pay four units, because if he accepts the cube at eight, he risks losing sixteen units if he does not bring in his last man within the next three or four throws. You were able to try for a gammon at no risk, planning to double only if, as in this game, White re-entered quickly with one of his men.

x The back game: retreat to victory

A SUCCESSFUL back game is based on a little luck and a lot of good technique. Back games often develop into exquisite duels of timing and position, and they are exciting because they provide the setting for dramatic turns in the fortunes of the players, with consequent turns of the doubling cube.

Some players who thrive on excitement seem deliberately to court the opportunity to establish a back game position. With proper timing and two or more points held deep in the opponent's home board, it is almost impossible for the opponent to bring his men off without leaving one or more shots. Indeed, were it not for the danger of being gammoned or even backgammoned, thus losing double or triple the face value of the cube, a back game would be equal in winning probability to any other game plan.

With the threat of gammon or backgammon in the wings, however, experts employ the back game as a strong line of retreat in the event of unsuccessful early gambling moves and blot-hitting contests. Note the generalship employed in the following game. Playing Red, as always, you try a series of gambling plays in the opening. White is able to hit repeatedly, forcing you into a back game. You must plan your campaign to maintain the two basic requisites for a successful back game:

1] Two points deep in your opponent's home board; and,

2] An imposing position in your own home board, to assure that when you do get your shot you are able to prevent the man you hit from escaping.

166

R1. 4 – 1

*Move a man to
your 9-point.
Move a man to
your 5-point.*

You (Red) elected the gambling move
in an effort to seize the 5-point quickly.

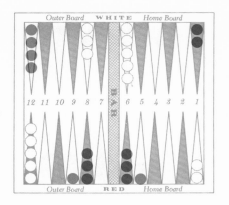

w1. 4 – 3

*Hit Red's blot
with the 4.
Move a builder to
the White 10-
point.*

White's throw enabled him to hit the
blot and bring a man to his 10-point as
a builder.

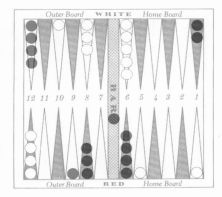

R2. 3 – 1

*Re-enter on the
White 3-point.
Hit the blot on
your 5-point.*

The 3–1 is usually an especially good
early throw since it would allow you to
make the 5-point. In this situation you
must waste part of your number re-entering the man from the bar. One danger
of being hit in the opening is that you
lose the opportunity to get the best out
of a subsequent good roll. You re-enter
on the 3-point and use the 1 to hit
White so as to prevent him from making
your 5-point.

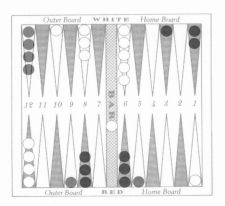

167

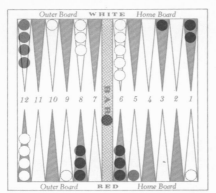

w2. 6 – 3
Re-enter on the 3-point and continue with the same man, hitting Red's blot.

White must re-enter on the 3-point but by continuing with this man, he is able to hit the Red builder on the 9-point.

r3. 4 – 2
Re-enter on the White 2-point. Hit White's blot in your outer board.

A 5–4 or 5–2 would have enabled you to come off the bar and make the 5-point. Unfortunately, this was not possible so you hit the White runner on your 9-point, partly to prevent its escape and partly to prevent White from utilizing his next throw to make a point. (Notice that if you did not have to re-enter you could have made your 4-point.)

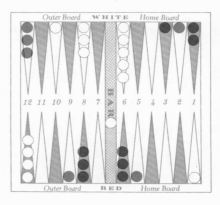

168

w3. 5 – 3

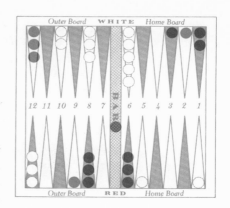

Re-enter on the 5-point, hitting Red's blot.

Cover the builder on the White 10-point.

White uses his 5–3 to good purpose by re-entering from the bar to hit Red's man on the 5-point and cover the builder on his 10-point. (Notice that if Red had not hit the White runner with the previous move, White's 5–3 could have made his 5-point, utilizing the builder on the 10-point.)

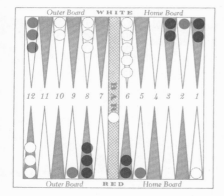

R4. 3 – 1

Re-enter on the 3-point.

Hit the White blot on your 5-point.

Needing to re-enter from the bar, you lose another number that would have made your 5-point. With so many men sent back to White's home board, you must get ready to play a back game. You re-enter with the 3 to preempt White's 3-point. Then, as with your previous throw, you hit White's blot on your 5-point continuing your attempt to prevent him from making key points on his next throw.

169

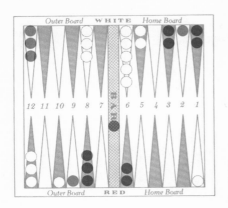

w4. 5 – 5

Re-enter and run out to the Red 10-point.

Make the White 5-point with the builders.

White's 5–5 does several things at once. Two of the 5s are used to "hit and run" while the other two make the 5-point, cashing in on having brought builders into his outer board.

EVALUATION AFTER WHITE'S 5–5

White's bombshell (5–5) removed any doubts you may have had about playing a back game. White enjoys an enormous lead in the race, plus a lead in the battle for valuable points. Red's future strategy will be based on controlling at least two points in White's home board. You will try to move your other men around the board as slowly as possible, meanwhile beginning to construct a good blockading position in your own home board in hopes of hitting a White blot later. To slow up your own movements, you will try to compel White to hit Red blots. White should try to avoid hitting these blots. He will try to immobilize the Red men in his home board for long enough to force you to break up your home board before you get a shot. One peculiarity of the back game is that, like an Irish horse race where each rides the other's horse and tries to finish last, both sides are trying to move as slowly as possible. As the game progresses, each side will jockey for position and timing.

R5. 5 – 4
Re-enter on the 4-point.
Run with the same man to the White 9-point.

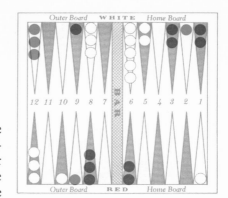

By moving a man from White's home board, you threaten to set up an additional blockading point in White's outer board. If you are allowed to establish the White 9-point, you will imperil the movement of White's men from your 12-point. If White hits either Red blot it will not disturb you; as the back game player, you are trying to move your men around the board slowly.

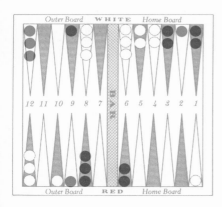

w5. 1 – 1
Move two men from the White 6-point to make the 4-point.

White's 1–1 is used to bring two men off his 6-point to make his 4-point, strengthening his blockade against Red's men in his home board.

R6. 4 – 3
Move a man from your 8-point and a man from your 9-point to make the 5-point.

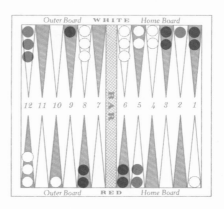

You cannot cover your blot on the 9-point with your man on the White 2-point since both the 4 and the 3 are blocked by White points. However, at last you are able to make your 5-point.

171

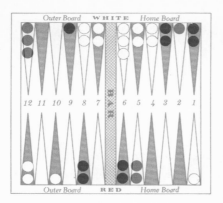

w6. 6 – 1

Move a man from the Red 12-point and a man from the White 8-point to make White's bar-point.

White's throw is near-perfect; making his bar-point gives him a 5-point blockade. (Making the bar-point is clearly better than hitting Red's blot, using the man from the Red 10-point.)

r7. 5 – 1

Move a man to your 11-point. Move a man to the White 3-point.

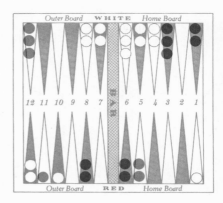

You do not want to hit White's blot, since that would slow up his movement. The 1 is a useful play, putting a man in position to move out with a 6 without giving up your 3-point. If you are not forced to move into your home board too quickly, you have a sound back game position.

POSITION AFTER RED'S 5–1

Before making his next throw, White doubles.

White has a good position but his double is premature. There is nothing wrong with Red's timing and White still has to bring his last runner to safety. Of course, you accept the double.

w7. 5 – 1

*Move a man to the
White 9-point.*

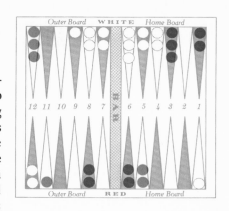

White brings his man from Red's 10-point to his 9-point, wisely choosing to use the 5 first to avoid the error of hitting a blot. Don't forget that White hopes Red will roll big numbers that will force the premature break-up of Red's home board. White purposely exposes to a direct shot. If this blot is hit, Red will be slowing White's movement which, as you've learned, is the wrong strategy. If the blot is not hit, White will try to cover this man, making the point that completes his prime.

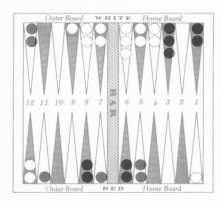

R8. 4 – 2

*Move a man from
the White 12-
point to your bar-
point.*

With this move, you are trying to force White to hit a blot; if not, you threaten to pen up White's runner and possibly force him to break his good advanced position.

w8. 4 – 3

*Move a man to the
White 9-point.
Move the runner
to Red's 4-point.*

White's roll is excellent. Without hitting Red, he is able to advance his runner and at the same time complete a prime.

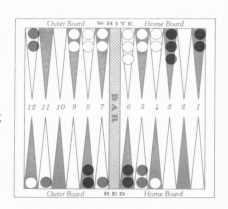

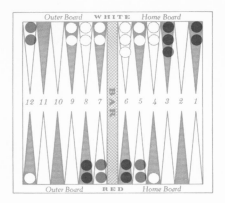

Move a man to your bar-point from your 11-point.

This seemingly innocuous move was made only after careful calculation. You have determined that you will not be forced to break your home board unless you are unfortunate enough to throw doublets. If this were not true, you would use the 3 to hit White's blot on your 4-point, hoping White would be forced to hit in return and slow you up.

w9. 6 – 5

Move the runner to the White 10-point.

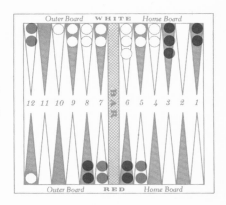

White runs out and "around the corner" with his runner. He is preparing to bring his men home.

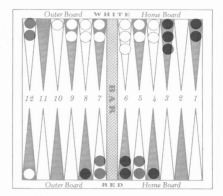

R10. 3 – 1

Move a man to your 4-point.

You begin to construct your home board by bringing a man from your 8-point to the 4-point. (Of course, you do not even consider hitting White's man on your 12-point. The last thing you want to do is slow him up.)

w10. 5 − 2

Move a man to the White 5-point. Move the runner to the White 11-point.

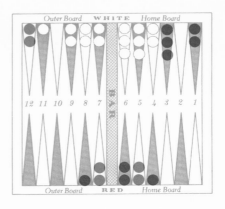

White moves his last blot out of reach with the 2 and uses the 5 to bring a man home. Notice that White chooses to bring home the man on the 10-point instead of the man on the 11-point. It is poor strategy to pile men on one home point; therefore, White diversifies the position of the men on his home board.

POSITION AFTER WHITE'S 5−2

White has now brought all of his men past your advance forces. His next job, to bring all of his men safely into his home board, is not as easy as it looks. Due to your blocking points, many numbers will prove awkward for him to play. You can expect your shot (or shots) soon, and should try to prepare a warm welcome for a White casualty by making consecutive points, preferably, of course, in your home board.

r11. 3 − 1

Cover your blot on the 4-point.

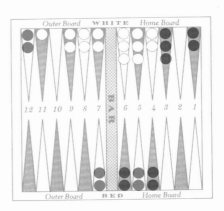

You are rolling well. Your last several throws have been small numbers. You continue your plan to make home board points, constructing your 4-point.

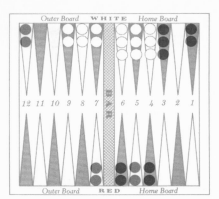

w11. 6 – 1
*Move the man
from the 11-point
to the 4-point.*

White plays the 6–1 in accordance with
the principal of diversification and brings
his outer man to his 4-point.

r12. 4 – 3
*Move your two
men from the
White 12-point to
your 9- and 10-
points.*

Bring two men down from the 12-point
to help in your point-building efforts.

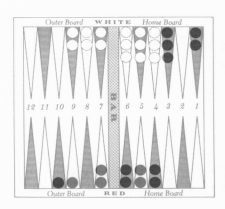

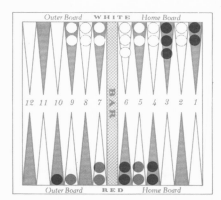

w12. 3 – 2
*Make the White
2-point by moving
men from the 5-
and 4-points.*

White makes the 2-point to provide another safe landing place for his men.
Notice how his earlier diversification enabled him to make the 2-point.

176

R*13. 5 – 2*

Move an outside man from your 10-point to your 3-point.

You continue to work toward constructing contiguous points in your home board by bringing a man to your 3-point.

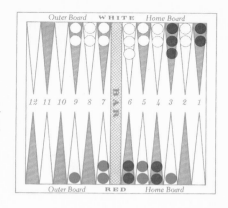

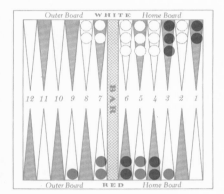

w13. 5 – 4

Move the two men from the 9-point to the 5- and 4-points.

White throws a good number. It allows him to bring his two back men home safely and neatly diversified.

R*14. 4 – 3*

Move a man to your 3-point.
Move a man to your 6-point.

Red makes his 3-point. He would have preferred to make this point with his blot on the 9-point, retaining the bar-point, or to have rolled a 6 so as to bring out the extra man from White's 3-point. But back game players cannot be choosy.

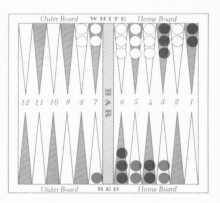

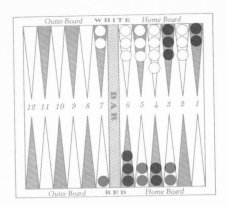

w14. 6 – 4

Move the two men from the 8-point to the 4- and 2-points.

White's 2-point, made on the twelfth move, now serves him in good stead by providing a landing place for the 6. The fact that this is the only way White can play 6–4 without leaving multiple shots is an indication that White is beginning to experience difficulties.

R15. 6 – 2

Move a man from the White 3-point to the 11-point.

You are unable to start the Red 2-point, so you liberate your extra man from White's home board. Your game is excellently timed.

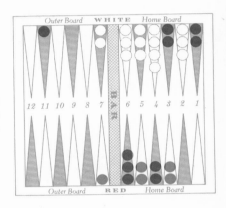

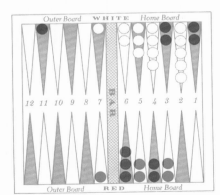

w15. 5 – 4

Move men from the 7- and 6-points to the 2-point.

There it is at last! White cannot play this move without leaving a shot. In fact, this is White's only legal play!

The odds favor your hitting the White blot: twenty numbers hit; sixteen numbers miss. If you hit the blot, the strength of your home board is enough to make you a probable winner. While 5–4 was an unfortunate throw for White, he was awkwardly placed and was in danger of leaving a double shot somewhere along the way.

Should you redouble? Absolutely not! Ownership of the cube is a solid advantage and you should not give it up in a situation as tenuous as this one. One thing is noteworthy, however. Nothing unusual happened, yet you are very much in the game. This is further evidence that White's earlier double was premature.

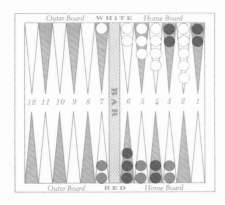

R16. 5 – 2
Move the man on the White 11-point to your bar-point.

And you miss the shot! So, you disappointedly move your loose man around the corner to build the bar-point. It is well that you did not relinquish ownership of the cube.

w16. 4 – 3
Move the White blot home and off the board.

White brings his blot to safety and bears off the same man from the 4-point. While he escaped the immediate shot, he still can't breathe easily; there are several hurdles yet to be overcome.

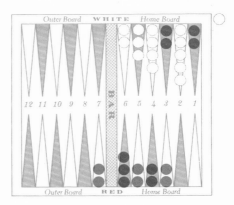

179

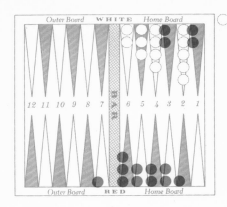

r17. 4 − 1
Move a man from your bar-point to your 2-point.

You prepare for another shot. Continue your plan for the orderly point-building process in your home board. (Do not move the man from your 6-point to your 1-point; even though you now give up a 5-point near prime.)

w17. 6 − 6
Bear off four men; two from the 6-point and two from the 5-point.

White's good throws in the early stages are balanced by a bad number which leaves a double shot on the 5-point. Other throws that might have left an immediate shot on this turn were 6–5 and 6–3.

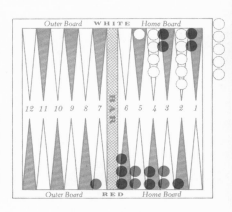

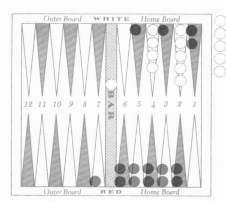

r18. 4 − 2
Hit White's blot with a man from his 3-point.
Make your 2-point.

And Red hits the blot. You had the happy choice of men to hit with and chose to hit with the 2 so as to be able to make the 2-point with the 4.

180

w18. 2 − 1

Re-enter on the 1-point.
Move a man from the White 4-point to the 2-point.

White is able to re-enter his man on the only open point on Red's home board, and to safely take the 2 by moving a man to his 2-point. Despite this lucky throw, he is living on borrowed time.

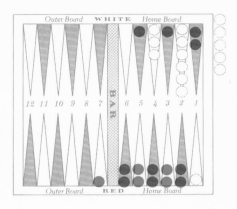

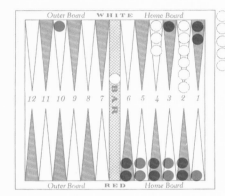

R19. 6 − 5

Hit the White blot from the bar-point.
Run out to the White 10-point.

White's hopes for survival revolve around being able to throw a 6 and escape your blockade. To reduce White's chances, you put him back on the bar, even though this leaves a blot on your 1-point. As a result, before White can try for a 31% chance to throw a 6 he must first throw a 1 to re-enter your home board, then a 6 to get out. You choose to take the 5 with Red's front man in order to bring you to your home board as quickly as possible, to cover the blot on your 1-point. You are not afraid that White will hit your blot, as White's home board is in ruins and presents no real threat to re-entry.

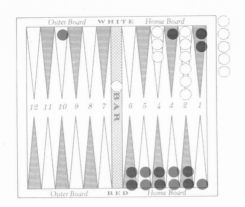

w19. 6 – 3

Fails to re-enter.

EVALUATION AFTER WHITE FAILS TO RE-ENTER.

As White has failed to re-enter, you redouble. The odds are greater than 2 to 1 against White's getting his man off the bar in one throw. Even if he does re-enter, White still has to roll a 6 to get out and then escape a battery of shots while trying to run around the board. With so many bridges to cross, White is more than a 3 to 1 underdog. He therefore refuses the double and pays two units rather than play a near hopeless position for four units.

Note that in the given position, you were virtually certain to close your board and bring off sufficient men before he could re-enter. In other words, he was far behind in a race, despite his five men already borne off. (A further factor to be considered is that, even if he succeeded in racing around the board the moment you opened a space, he would miss every time he threw a 1.) Had he already borne eight men off, however, the odds would be too close to warrant a redouble until you had established a position and borne off two or three men while he was still on the bar. It is important that you re-double at the earliest proper moment, for two reasons: First, if you wait too long there is no chance your opponent will take it. Second, you should not give him a free ride; if he needs a near-miracle to win, he should be made to pay for the privilege of keeping that chance alive.

The only real error in this game was White's handling of the doubling cube. A positional game or a back game should be doubled only when a clear defect can be seen in the opponent's set-up. White had no indication at the time he doubled that Red would not be able to maintain his home board or the blocking points in the White home board.

As it turned out, White's premature turn of the cube resulted in his losing twice what he would otherwise have lost in this game.

182

XI Backgammon variants
(including the new "Roll-over")

BACKGAMMON, like so many of our best games, derives from the near Eastern and Oriental cultures. Different sets of rules have been played in different countries on the same board. The evolution of backgammon is marked by romantic game titles such as Moultezim, Plakoto, and Gioul. In our own society, the game of Acey-Deucey was popular among Navy personnel during the Second World War. We will not become involved in the rules of these generally obsolete games. Instead, let's discuss popular variations on the basic rules including the newest and most revolutionary idea, "The Roll-over."

The automatic double

AS YOU KNOW, the privilege of making the first move is won by the player who throws the highest die. Some contestants add some spice by agreeing that whenever the same number is thrown by both players, the cube is automatically turned to 2, thus doubling the stake of that particular game. In theory, the cube may be turned each time the same number is thrown by both sides; that is, if the players throw the same number twice, the cube would start at 4, if they throw the same number three times, the cube would start at 8, and so on. In practice, most players who use this rule limit themselves to one automatic double per game.

The gammon cube

ANOTHER common variant provides that a gammon does not count unless the cube has been turned at least once; that is, one player must have doubled his opponent. (An automatic double does not satisfy this requirement since when a game is doubled automatically, the cube remains in the middle.) In other words, one side or the other must *own the cube* at the time of the gammon for it to be scored as

183

a double game. This rule tends to eliminate the long game in which one side's position is hopeless (so that if offered a double he will decline), wherefore the opponent continues play in hopes that he can achieve a gammon or backgammon.

The chouette

CHOUETTE is a method that allows more than two people to play at once. To begin a chouette, each person throws a die. The player who throws the highest die is "in the box" and plays against all the others. The person who throws the second highest die becomes the *captain* of the remaining group, and plays for them. The order of finish of the first throw is noted; ties are broken by having those players who are tied roll again.

The man in the box plays for the stake of the game against each of the other players; that is, if the game is being played for one dollar, and the chouette consists of five people, he is playing for four dollars — one dollar against each of his opponents.

The partners may consult against the man in the box on both the movement of the men and whether or not to double. In the event of a disagreement, the captain has the final say on what move to make and whether the cube should be turned. The only time that consultation is not permitted is when the man in the box doubles or redoubles. His opponents, in order of their precedence, accept or decline as individuals and the man in the box scores against the players who declined and plays on against those players who accept. Players who accept advance in precedence over those who decline. Needless to say, once a player declines a double, he may not offer any further opinions or advice during that game.

At the end of a game (or during a game if the captain declines a double) the next player in line becomes the captain. The captain takes the place of the man in the box if the box loses. Each player's score is kept individually.

If the game is played with automatic doubles, the man in the box has the option of whether to allow the automatic double or to play at the original stake. The gammon cube rule is very desirable in a chouette since it speeds up the game; after all, who wants to wait on the outside while a player laboriously tries to negotiate an undoubled gammon.

THIS VARIANT allows the sound backgammon player to punish the overaggressive doubler. If you have been doubled in a position where you feel that the doubler does not have a real advantage, you may redouble and still retain possession of the cube *if you redouble before your opponent throws the dice.* This option is called a *beaver.* As an example, consider the racing game on page 136. White's double was so premature, that you would be justified to *beaver* his double by turning the cube to 4 before he throws the dice. In a chouette, beavers are individual just as accepting the cube or not is individual. Differences of opinion are common in chouettes. I have seen situations in a four-handed chouette where the man in the box doubled and one opponent declined the cube, one opponent accepted the cube, and the other opponent beavered!

WITH THE increasing popularity of backgammon, international tourneys were the inevitable outcome. The two contestants play until one or the other reaches a predetermined number of points. When this happens, the one who gets there first is declared the winner of the match and eliminates his opponent. Such a match is most often for 11 points, though the finals of a tournament may be a match of 25 points. The longer the match, the less chance there is for an inferior player to win. None of the previously mentioned variants are used in match play; no automatic doubles, no beavers, and it is legal and often desirable to play for an undoubled gammon. The only rule is that if one side is one point away from victory, the cube may not be turned for one game.

The strategy of match play is based on whether you are ahead or behind in the match and revolves around the doubling cube. If you are behind, you will tend to double in unclear positions while if you are ahead, you will tend to be very conservative with the cube. As the final games of a match are reached, the cube is used indiscriminately, based completely upon the score. As an example, assume that your opponent has just won a game bringing his total to 10 in an 11 point match. You have only 8 points and, according to the rules of match play, you may not double for one game. You win a close race bringing the score to 10–9. In the next game, you win the first move with 6–1, making the bar-point. Your opponent throws 5–1 and plays it in the recommended fashion. You double the game automatically since the only object is to reach the magic number of 11 points. Surprisingly enough, your opponent should decline the double, hoping for a better start in the opening. The score would now be 10–10 and

185

of course, the cube becomes superfluous since the winner of the next game will win the match.

Match play is the most skillful form of play. Proof of this is that seldom does a "dark horse" win a backgammon tournament. The best players will usually meet in the finals.

A TYPICAL KNOCK OUT TOURNAMENT

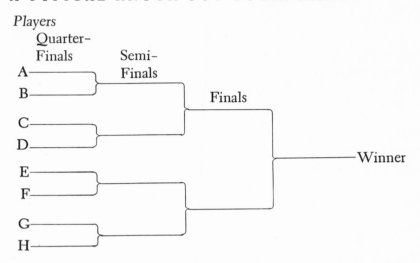

This diagram shows the quarter finals of a tournament. The winner of the match between players A and B plays the winner of the match between players C and D, while the winner of the match between E and F plays the winner of the match between G and H. The losers are eliminated. The two winners of this semifinal match play against each other in the finals to determine a final winner.

The New "Roll-over"

MOST OF THE INNOVATIONS in games are of unknown origin. For example, no one knows who first suggested the doubling cube — the brilliant inspiration that radically changed the game, quickened its pace, increased its excitement and contributed more than anything else to the present popularity of backgammon. So, let it be recorded for history that *Roll-over* — perhaps the first idea since the doubling cube that is likely to have a profound effect on backgammon — was the brainchild of my old friend and associate, Richard L. Frey. I can even tell you how it came about.

A part of the "joy" of backgammon is the privilege of moaning

186

and groaning when you make a poor throw or when your opponent makes an exceptionally lucky one. If you've played fairly often, undoubtedly an opponent has anwered your groan with a mocking, "Would you like (me) to roll it over?" This very taunt set Dick Frey to thinking about what might happen if a player had the right to answer, "Yes" just once in each game. So, since it was a family game, he and his wife tried it out. The result was little short of sensational. From their experience and that of others who first tried it comes these simple rules:

Once in any game, each player has the right to say "Roll-over" after he or his opponent has thrown the dice. The previous roll is cancelled and the player rolls again. The opponent may, on the same turn or on any later turn, use his own "Roll-over" privilege, provided he has not already done so.

What had started out as merely a release from aggravation proved to have a profound effect on total strategy.

For example, the player who retains his Roll-over privilege after his opponent has already used it has a big advantage and can properly double in an otherwise virtually even position. Under these circumstances, his opponent must be wary of accepting a double.

Hence, the right to exercise the Roll-over privilege should be reserved as long as possible. On the other hand, whenever your roll has been so bad, or your opponent's roll so good that you are certain to be doubled and will just as certainly resign, you may as well call on your Roll-over then and there. Or the same decision may be made when your throw would force you to break up an advantageous position in a game where you are ahead, or has failed to hit one of several opposing blots when you can expect to achieve a big advantage — perhaps a wipe out position — with a reasonably good throw.

If you are able to reserve your Roll-over until both sides are bearing off, you can expect to achieve or to consolidate a tremendous advantage, or to equalize a tremendous disadvantage. Consider this simple example:

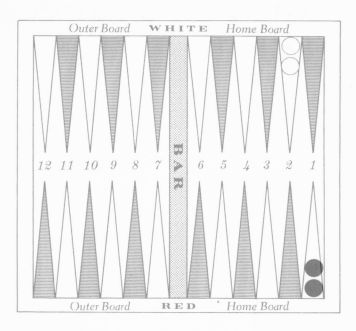

Outer Board   **W H I T E**   Home Board

12   11   10   9   8   7   **B A R**   6   5   4   3   2   1

Outer Board   **R E D**   Home Board

It is White's turn. In the chapter dealing with the cube, we demonstrated that, although White should double, you (Red) should accept because by doing so you are accepting odds of 3-to-1, whereas White is only a 2.6 to 1 favorite. However, playing under the Roll-over rule, if you still have your option and White has used his, he should not double. He needs to avoid throwing a 1 in two consecutive rolls; if he does not throw a 1 the first time, you will demand that he roll over.

Although the Roll-over adds a new dimension of skill to play in all games, it is particularly satisfying in a family or sociable game, where it can be used as a handicap system; for example, giving the weaker player an extra Roll-over or eliminating the privilege for the stronger player.

Experience dictates the need for each player to start the game holding a marker or counter which represents his Roll-over opportunity and which he must surrender at the time he uses it; otherwise, questions will arise whether or not the option has yet been used. Another suggestion: it should not be necessary for a player to call Roll-over before an opponent has completed his move.

It is also a good idea to adopt the rule that when one player exercises his Roll-over option to compel his opponent to roll again, the opponent may not double until his next turn.

I cannot guarantee that "Roll-over" will make backgammon less aggravating all the time. It can be frustrating to throw a "miracle" roll, only to have it called back. However, I would certainly suggest that you adopt the rule and give it a trial in friendly social games.

ACEY-DEUCEY

This game, which is very similar to classical backgammon, gained most of its popularity among U.S. Navy personnel during World War II. The difference is that the smallest number on the dice (ace-deuce) carries a massive bonus in that not only is the 1–2 moved, the player chooses and then moves any doublet he sees fit and then throws again. Among unsophisticated players, backgammon is considered nothing more than a race, and on that basis, 1–2 is a "hopeless throw." The atom bomb aspect of the ace-deuce played this way changes the odds drastically and reduces the level of skill; there is more room for the lucky throw. The following is an example of an acey-deucy "atom bomb."

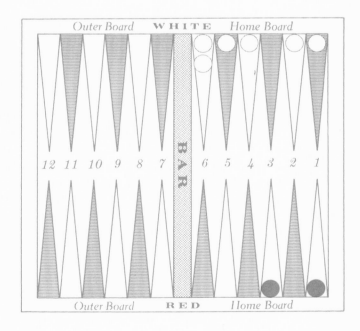

It is White's turn and he throws 2–1. He plays the 2–1 by removing two men and chooses 6–6 as his doublet, removing his last four men and winning the game. The general logic of a backgammon race is that the best numbers are also the rarest. Yet, in this case, 6–6 (a 35 to 1 shot) does not help White, while 2–1 (a 17 to 1 shot) will win the game. This illogical quality is an example of why backgammon is a superior game to acey-deucey.

xii Handicaps

ANY skillful activity has levels of competency that are dependent upon knowledge and experience. Backgammon is no exception to this rule. The stronger or more experienced player has an advantage over his weaker counterpart, though, at the expert level, the difference can be very small indeed. The increasing popularity of backgammon as a family game makes handicaps a must. How frustrating for the wife who learns backgammon from the husband, or the child who learns from mother, to lose constantly. After about a week of this, the student will more than likely give up the game in favor of some less aggravating pastime. Consider the idea of adjusting the odds by giving a handicap.

In a handicap system, the more experienced player starts out with a prearranged disadvantage to give both sides a fair chance to win. This has a twofold advantage. First, it gives the novice a reasonable opportunity to taste the encouragement of the fruits of victory. Second, there is added incentive for the weaker player, conscious of his growing skill, to force the stronger player to reduce the handicap by demonstrating his ability to win consistently.

The following is a suggested list of handicaps starting from the smallest possible disadvantage.

1] FIRST THROW — The weaker player shakes the dice and makes the first move without choosing for the privilege, thus starting with a slight initiative. Conventionally doublets are disallowed, though you may agree to allow doublets.

2] ASSIGNED FIRST THROW — Instead of a random throw, the weaker player is assigned a good first number. The three common assigned numbers in ascending order are:

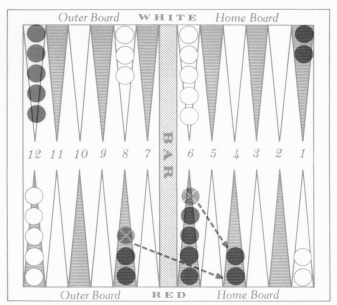

a] **4 – 2**
Allowing the weaker player to make his 4-point.

b] **6 – 1**
Allowing the weaker player to make his bar-point.

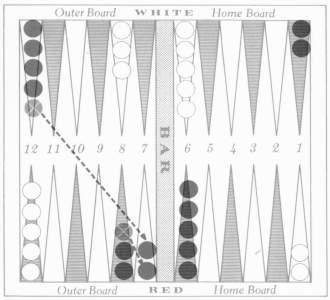

c] **1 – 1**

Allowing the weaker player to make both his bar-point and his 5-point.

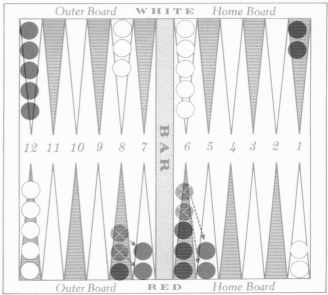

3] THE CUBE — The weaker player starts with ownership of the cube; that is, he is the only one permitted to double the game initially. Once a player has learned the elements of deployment, this handicap assures him of a terrific advantage.

Between equal players, the owner of the cube would be at least a 2 to 1 favorite

4] EXTRA ROLL-OVERS — The best form of handicap. The weaker player may have one, two, three, four or more Roll-over options than his stronger and more resourceful opponent. The more disparity between the players, the more Roll-over options the weaker player receives. The superiority of this handicap structure becomes clear to the extent that advantages of different degree can be conferred exclusively within the framework of the Roll-over. (See "The Roll-over;" page 186.)

XIII The sad tale of my consultant

Inevitably you will meet the unfortunate player who throws the worst possible dice . . . or so he claims. If you are inclined to listen, he will regale you with any number of hard luck stories about how he would have won the game except for his impossibly unlucky throws or his opponent's impossibly lucky ones. Admittedly, I have little patience with these people who never remember their good dice and forever complain about their bad dice, but the hard luck story told to me by Chuck Papazian must evoke the sympathy of the hardest of hearts.

Chuck walked into the club and slumped into a chair. "That's it," he said. "I am going to give up backgammon forever after what happened to me this afternoon."

Since Chuck is not usually a hard-luck-story teller, I invited him to continue.

"We both had brought all of our men into our home board. I was 15 pips ahead, 75 to 90, so of course I doubled."

"Yes, yes," I replied slightly disappointed, "he accepted the double and threw a series of doublets to beat you."

"Wrong," said Chuck, "he only threw one doublet. As a matter of fact I threw two doublets."

"So what are you complaining about?" I asked.

"Oh nothing," smiled Chuck sadly, "it's just that my 15 pip lead plus my extra doublet was insufficient for me to avoid being *gammoned!*"

The story of this extraordinary game:

In this bizarre situation where White has 15 men on the 6-point and Red has 15 men on the 5-point, neither side is very proud of their diversification. Still, 15 pips are 15 pips and Chuck duly turned the cube and White accepted.

To follow this story set up the board in its original position and play out the indicated moves.

194

R*1.* 4 – 2

w*1.* 6 – 2

Chuck (Red) makes his only legal play by moving two men from his 5-point to the 3- point and 1-point.

White removes a man from his 6-point and drops a man to his 4-point — the only legal play.

 R2. 4 – 2

w2. 6 – 1

Again, Chuck is unable to remove a man so he moves two more men from his 5-point to the 3-point and the 1-point.

White removes another man from his 6-point and diversifies as best he can by dropping a man to his 5-point.

 R3. 4 – 2

w3. 6 – 3

Still unable to begin bearing off, Chuck moves two more men from his 5-point to the 3-point and 1-point. Once is happenstance, twice is coincidence, but three times is enemy action from Lady Luck. With this in mind, Chuck calls in good-natured fashion for new dice.

White removes a man from his 6-point and continues to diversify by moving a man to his 3-point.

R4. 4 – 2

 w4. 5 – 4

"These new dice don't seem to help," smiled Chuck to no one in particular. Having plenty of practice with this number, it took him no time at all to move two men from his 5-point to his 3-point and 1-point.

Diversification pays off for White, as he is able to remove the two men from his 5-point and 4-point.

 R5. 4 – 2

w5. 6 – 3

"Can somebody please bring me a pair of dice that do not have a one-track mind?" groaned a mildly irritated Chuck. Needless to say Chuck moved two men from his 5-point to his 3-point and his 1-point.

White removes two more men from the board. Being a nice guy, even he began to sympathize with Chuck's plight.

 R6. 4 – 2

w6. 6 – 5

We will draw the curtain of charity over Chuck's mood as he rolls his sixth 4–2 in a row. He moves two more men from his 5-point to his 3-point and 1-point.

White removes another man from his 6-point and makes the only other legal play by shifting a man from his 6-point to his 1-point.

196

R7. 4 – 2   w7. 6 – 1

"If I don't throw a different number soon," said Chuck quietly, "I will say or do something very ungentlemanly." Of course he moved two men from his 5-point to his 3-point and 1-point.

White removes his two men from his 6-point and his 1-point.

R8. 2 – 2   w8. 4 – 2

"I don't believe it," exclaimed Chuck, "I actually threw a different number." Of course he was still unable to remove a man from the board so he moved his man on the 5-point and two men from his 3-point to his already overcrowded 1-point.

Chuck's nightmare number does not faze White as he removes a man from his 6-point.

R9. 2 – 2   w9. 6 – 6

Chuck is in a new rut! He makes his only legal move by shifting four men from the 3-point to his 1-point. At last no matter how horrible his next number is, Chuck will be able to move a man. However. . . .

And White clears the board and scores a gammon.

"How come you forgot to redouble?" mumbled Chuck like a man in shock.

"And miss my chance for a gammon?" his opponent grinned.

"Some chance," Chuck grumbled. "Disregarding your highly efficient throws, the odds against what happened are exactly 502,053,-031,925 to 1."

Let me say that I don't really believe this story. But until I hear a better one, I must consider it the king of the hard luck tales.

P.S. You will be happy to know that Chuck did not give up playing. Despite its not infrequent tribulations, backgammon is definitely and pleasurably habit forming.

Laws of Modern Backgammon

Based on those promulgated by Racquet and Tennis Club, New York. Additions in brackets [ ] reflect alterations or amplifications generally followed in modern play.

THE GAME

1. The game of Backgammon is played by two persons.

2. Thirty men — fifteen of one color and fifteen of another — are used, and are set up as shown on page 3, on a standard board, of four quarters or tables having six points each.

3. For entering and throwing off, the points in both inner tables are considered as numbered from 1 to 6, beginning with the point nearest the light. [As you will observe from the comment regarding diagram 2 in this book, suggesting that you turn it upside down, the home tables may be on either side of the board, and the position of the light may or may not be a deciding factor.]

4. Direction of play is from adversary's inner table to adversary's outer table, to player's outer table, and then to player's inner (home) table.

5. Play of the men is governed by two dice, thrown (cast) from a cup in which the dice are shaken before casting.

6. Choice of seats, men, set up, dice, etc., shall be made by the player winning the open throw. [As played today, before the start of any subsequent game, either player may ask to mix the dice. All four dice are then cast from one cup and each player chooses one die in turn, first choice going to the opponent.]

THE THROWS

7. For the opening throw each player throws a single die. Every tie requires another opening throw. Whoever throws the higher number wins,

and for his first move plays the numbers upon both dice. After that each player in turn throws two dice.

8.   The dice must be rolled together and come to rest flat (not "cocked") upon the tables at the player's right, otherwise they must be thrown again.

9.   If a throw is made before an adversary's play is completed, or if either player touches a die before it has come to rest, the adversary of the offender may require a rethrow. [In practice, this law is deemed to require that the dice *must* be rethrown.]

10.   The player must leave his dice upon the board until his play is completed. Should he pick them up or turn them over before the completion of his play, the adversary may declare the play void and require the offender to replace the man or men moved and to throw again. [If a player picks up his dice before completing his move, his adversary may require or forbid the uncompleted portion of the move. A move is deemed accepted as taken if the adversary casts the dice for his next turn, even if his cast results in cocked dice.]

THE PLAY

11.   The play of the men consists:
    A] In moving a man the exact number of points indicated by the number on a die thrown. [One man may be moved as indicated by the face of each of the two dice, or two may be moved, each in accordance with the number faced on a single die (more than two if the number thrown is a doublet) provided that no man touches down — even in passing — on a point held by his opponent.]
    B] Entering a man, in the adversary's inner table, on a point corresponding to the number on a die thrown.
    c] Bearing off a man in player's inner table — when no man is left outside that table or on the bar — from a point corresponding to the number on a die thrown, or as provided in Law 15.
    Doublets require four plays — if possible — of the die number thrown.

12.   No play may be made which lands on a point held by two or more of the adversary's men.

13.   When a play lands on a single man (blot) of the adversary's, such man is "hit," and must be lifted and placed on the bar for entry in the player's inner table.

14.   A player having a man on the bar may not play until that man has been entered.

15.   Plays must be made for both dice if possible. Either number may be played first. If only one number can be played, and there is a choice, the higher must be played.

In bearing off, a man may at all times be correctly borne off from the highest occupied point which is lower than the number indicated by a die. If a number is thrown for an unoccupied point, no man below can be thrown off, for such number, while any man remains on a higher point.

16.   Whenever a man has been moved correctly and quitted (the player's hand removed), that play cannot be changed. [This law is not now followed. Instead, a player may alter his moves until he has picked up his dice, thereby ending his turn.]

ERRORS

17.   If an error has been made in the set-up, either player may correct it prior to the completion of his first play.

18.   If an error in play has been made, either player may require its correction before a subsequent throw, but not thereafter. The man played in error must be correctly played if possible.

SCORING

19.   A game is won by the player who first bears off all of his men. A gammon (double game) is won if the adversary has not borne off a single man. This doubles the count.

A backgammon (triple game) is won if the adversary has not borne off a single man, and has one or more men in the winner's inner table or upon the bar. This triples the count.

20.   *Doubling Game.* The count is raised:
Automatically
By agreement, each tie of the opening throw may either:
A] Double the previous count.
B] Add one to the previous count.
Unless an understanding has been reached as to the method and limitation of automatic raises they are not played.
Voluntarily
Either player may offer the first optional double of the previous count. After that the right to double the previous count alternates, being always with the player who has accepted the last double.

A double may be offered only when it is the player's turn to play and before he has thrown the dice [even if he rolls cocked dice]. A double may be accepted or declined. The refusal of a double terminates the game, and the player refusing loses whatever the count may amount to at that time. Gammons and Backgammons double or triple the last count.

21. BY AGREEMENT other methods of scoring may be used, such as: *The Point Game*. In this 1 point is scored, by the winner of a game, for each man left in the adversary's inner table; 2 points are scored for each man left in the adversary's outer table; 3 points for each man left in the winner's outer table, and 4 points for each man left in the winner's inner table or upon the bar. [This scoring method is obsolete.]

CHOUETTE

1. Chouette is played by three or more members.

2. In beginning the game each member shall throw a die and the one throwing the highest number is then the "Man in the Box," the next highest is the "Captain." The other members, in accordance with each one's throw, rank below the Captain and succeed him in that order.

3. The initial throw shall determine each member's position but in the event of a tie, only those tying throw again for their position. The highest or higher number always has precedence.

4. Any applicant to Chouette may be accepted. He becomes the last ranking member in the first game in which he participates.

5. After the positions have been determined the Man in the Box and the Captain proceed as in the two handed game except that all the remaining members are partners of the Captain.

6. The Man in the Box plays alone and scores separately with each one of his adversaries. He retains his position until defeated. In such event, he retires as a player and takes his place as the last ranking member (unless there be an added member). The Captain then becomes the Man in the Box.

7. The Captain may consult with any or all of the partners on any question that may arise in the course of the game. He is, however, the final arbiter, except as hereafter provided. Should he be defeated, he loses his position and takes his place as last ranking member (unless there be an added member). The highest ranking partner then becomes Captain. [The Captain's decision as to a play or doubling the Man in the Box is final and is binding on all members of his side. By custom, however, if there are more than two players on his side, the Captain does not offer a double

202

or redouble unless his decision is concurred in by one other member of his side.]

8. A double offered by the Man in the Box may be refused by any partner. Each rejector forfeits to the Man in the Box his count previous to the proposed double.

9. Should the Captain decline to accept a double offered by the Man in the Box he loses his position, and forfeits to the Man in the Box his count previous to the proposed double.

10. When a double has been declined by the Captain, any or all of the other members may accept it. The highest ranking of those accepting becomes Captain until the termination of that game.

11. Accepting or declining a double does not change the rank of the member; except that declining by the Captain loses him that position even though the game be eventually won by the accepting partners.

Glossary

Automatics   An optional rule whereby the cube is automatically turned to 2 if both players throw the same number while contesting for the opening move.

Back Game   A strategic plan whereby one player establishes points in his opponent's home board in the expectation of being able to hit one of his opponent's men while his opponent is attempting to bring his men home.

Backgammon   The name of the game. Also, the result of a game in which one player has removed all of his men while his opponent still has a man (or men) in the winner's home board. This counts as a triple game.

Back man/men   See Runner. Also, the rear-most men at any time.

Bar   The center divider separating the outer boards from the home boards. Hit blots are placed "on the bar" to be re-entered in the opponent's home board on a subsequent throw.

Bar-point   The 7-point. One of the key blocking points.

Bearing off   The process of removing the men from the board. The final stage of the game.

Beaver   An optional rule whereby a doubled player may demand that the stakes be quadrupled instead of doubled, while retaining possession of the cube. This demand must be made before the doubler has thrown.

Blockade   A series of contiguous points designed to inhibit the movements of your opponent's men. The most common blockade is directed against the opposing runners and usually involves the control of one or both of the key points.

Blocking Game   A strategy in which one or both players base their deployment on impeding the movement of the opponent's men.

Blot   A single man on a point. A blot can be hit by an opposing man and placed upon the bar.

Board   The entire playing surface. Also, any one of the four quadrants of the board; your home board, the opponent's home board, your outer board, and your opponent's outer board.

Box   In a Chouette, the player who is playing against the rest of the contestants. Such a player is said to be "in the box." (See Chouette.)

Builder   A man whose function it is to aid in the future acquisition of important points.

Captain   In a Chouette, the player who represents the interests of all the contestants who are playing against the man in the box (see Chouette).

Checkers   See Men.

Chouette   A game of backgammon composed of three or more players. One player, said to be "in the box," plays against the captain. The fortunes of the other players depend on the fortunes of the captain. The various partners may consult freely against the man in the box. At the conclusion of a game, the captain's place is taken by the next-in-order of the contestants on his side, who becomes the new captain. The box plays for the agreed stake against each of his opponents.

Contact Game   Any position where the opposing positions restrain each other's movements. Contact games are usually some form of positional games and may require delicate maneuvering to maintain an equal balance.

Counters   See Men.

Counting the pips   A method of calculating how a player stands in a race by determining the minimum number of pips he will have to roll to remove all of his men from the board. By comparing his total pip count to his opponent's total pip count, he can determine whether he is ahead or behind.

Cube   The doubling cube. A die-shaped object with a geometric progression of six numbers ranging from 2 to 64. At the outset of a game, the cube is placed in the middle; that is, either player has the option of doubling the game. The player who is doubled or redoubled has the option of declining or accepting the cube. If he declines, he loses automatically; if he accepts, the stakes are doubled. The cube is then placed nearer to him, indicating that he is now the owner of the cube and is the only one who can next redouble. (See Double.)

Dice Cup   A cylinder or open-ended box, in which a player shakes his dice, and from which he casts them.

Direct Shot   A chance to hit a blot that is within 6 pips of an opposing man. This blot can therefore be hit by a number on a single die.

Double   The process of turning the cube. Each double multiplies the preceding stakes by two. While the cube itself has markings only up to 64, theoretically doubling and redoubling can continue beyond this

206

number. In practical play, however, a serious game is seldom redoubled and played beyond 8.

Doublet   A throw producing the same number of pips on both dice, entitling the shooter to twice his normal move. Also called *"Doubles."*

Doubling Cube   See Cube.

Exposed Man   See Blot.

Gammon   A game in which one player removes all of his men before his opponent has removed any. This scores as a double game. If, in addition, the loser still has a man in the winner's home board, he loses a triple game. (See Backgammon).

Inner Table   See Home Board.

Half a roll   The number of pips on one die. A player who has been hit must waste half a roll to re-enter a man from the bar.

Handicap   A concession by which the stronger player accepts a predetermined disadvantage before play begins, so as to help equalize the winning chances for both sides.

Hit   A move which lands on an opponent's exposed man, thus placing that man on the bar.

Home Board   The quadrant to which a player must move all of his men before bearing off.

Home Table   See Home Board.

Indirect Shot   An exposed man (or blot) that can be hit only by a combination number using both of the opponent's dice. (By definition, this blot is seven or more pips away from an opposing man.) Also, the opportunity to hit or the act of hitting such a blot.

Key Points   The bar-point and the 5-point, referred to as key points because they are the most effective points to restrain the opposing runners.

Lover's Leap   The move of one runner from the 1-point to immediate safety on the 12-point, made possible by the throw of 6–5.

Men   The individual soldiers of a player's army. Each side has fifteen men, occasionally referred to as *checkers, counters, stones* or *tiles.*

Non-Contact Game   The race. Both armies have effectively side-stepped any opposing restraint and their sole object is to move around the track with maximum economy, bringing all the men home. Once there, each side tries to complete the bearing off process as quickly as possible.

Off the Board   Said of those men already removed from the board during the bearing off process.

On the Bar   See Bar.

Outer Board   The quadrant immediately adjacent to the home board. The last board a player must pass through to reach his home board.

Outer Table   See Outer Board.

Pips   The dots that appear on the face of the die, denoting the value of that face.

Points   Spaces occupied by two or more men. A point controls that particular space, preventing an opponent from touching down on it with one of his men. Also, the designation of a location on the board; e.g., the 5-point, the 8-point, the bar-point, etc.

Prime   Six contiguous points occupied by one side. A prime prevents the movement of an opposing man if that opposing man is trapped behind the prime.

Race   See Running Game.

Re-enter   The process required to bring a hit man from the bar to a point in the opponent's home board. To re-enter, a player must throw a number on one of his dice that represents a point not controlled by his opponent. Re-entering must be accomplished before any other move can be made. If a player fails to throw a number that will allow him to re-enter, he loses his turn and must try again to re-enter on his next legal turn.

Roll-over   An optional method of play whereby each side has one chance during the game to either re-cast the dice or demand that his opponent do so. This variation is particularly well suited for family play, especially if an experienced player is teaching an inexperienced player.

Runners   The two men that start the game on the 1-point in the opponent's home board. The runners have the longest distance to move to reach their own home board and are most vulnerable to blockades. Also called *back men*.

Running Game   A strategy whereby a player tries to move his men home as quickly as possible, avoiding blockades and counter blockades as much as he can. The Race.

Safe   A position or play that exposes no men to being hit.

Settlement   An agreement to end the game based on potential equity, rather than put the stakes "up for grabs" based on a single fortuitous throw of the dice.

Straight Race   A position where both sides have bypassed their opponent's blockaders and are preoccupied solely with moving their men home and bearing off as quickly as possible; a running game.

Wipeout   An aggressive game plan where one side tries to keep his opponent off balance by simultaneously hitting blots (usually runners) and making home board points. If successful, this stratagem can lead to a gammon. If unsuccessful, a very badly timed positional game may result. Practical chances are about equal.